NORTH to LAKE SUPERIOR

CHARLES W. PENNY — *a photograph of an original portrait, circa 1840, owned by Mr. Gregory Harrier.*

NORTH to LAKE SUPERIOR

The Journal of
CHARLES W. PENNY
1840

Edited by
JAMES L. CARTER
and
ERNEST H. RANKIN

THE JOHN M. LONGYEAR RESEARCH LIBRARY
Marquette, Michigan
1970

Library of Congress Catalog Card Number 71-111886

First Printing, February, 1970
Second Printing, March, 1971
Third Printing, December, 1976

Printed and bound in U.S.A.
THE BOOK CONCERN, INC., HANCOCK, MICHIGAN 49930

Foreword

One of the fringe benefits from writing books is the frequently fascinating letters the writer gets from his readers—especially those letters *unaccompanied* by five-pounds of tattered manuscript and a wistful suggestion that the writer please kindly drop everything and get it in shape for publication! Of all my published books perhaps none elicited more interesting letters than those I got following upon the publication of my historical novel, *Laughing Whitefish.*

That story, one may recall, was a fictional account of the first discovery of iron ore in the Lake Superior region at Negaunee in the autumn of 1844 and which later became the site of the fabulously successful Jackson Mine; of the litigation that followed in which Charlotte Kawbawgam, daughter of a Chippewa Indian called Marji Gesick, sought to collect her share of the fractional interest promised but never paid her father for guiding Philo M. Everett and his party of Jackson business men to the discovery site; and of the successful conclusion years later of that litigation, which was handled by Frederick Owen Clark (1843-1905), brilliant lawyer grandfather of Robert Harlow Clark, appropriately enough himself today a lawyer and also a member and director of the Marquette County Historical Society.

One of the more interesting of these letters I got was from Gregory Harrier of Berkeley, California whose grandfather Charles W. Penny, Mr. Harrier wrote me, had travelled in the Upper Peninsula in the summer of 1840 along with Douglass Houghton and had kept a detailed journal of his trip —and would I like to read it? I would, I wrote back, and in due course the yellowed and faded original journal arrived and

I promptly read it and found it fascinating. In fact I at once discerned that the journal constituted a real historical scoop, and I so wrote Mr Harrier.

Would I like to keep the journal? Mr. Harrier wrote back, whereupon I wrote him that while I much appreciated his generosity I felt the journal was far too valuable a document to get buried in my chaotic filing system and suggested that he give it to the Marquette County Historical Society where it would not only be safe but available to far more people.

Mr. Harrier generously agreed with my suggestion and so the journal now reposes in the vaults of the Society at Marquette. What follows is the full text of that journal for the first time exposed to public view since it was written 'way back when such giants of Michigan history as Douglass Houghton and William Burt were still alive. Perhaps it will help recapture some of the flavor and romance of those bygone days.

John D. Voelker (Robert Traver)

Ishpeming, Michigan
May 20, 1969

Acknowledgments

Our first thanks for the use of the Charles W. Penny journal should undoubtedly go to John D. Voelker. It was he who encouraged Mr. Gregory Harrier of Berkeley, California, Penny's grandson, to present this extraordinary heirloom to the John M. Longyear Research Library of the Marquette County Historical Society. Our thanks are equally sincere to Mr. Harrier who has brought to light and made possible for publication an important document on Lake Superior history.

Although Penny was an excellent penman, he wrote in the style of over a century ago, and it required long, arduous hours for Mrs. Richard A. Weesen, research assistant of the Society, to make the typewritten transcription. We are grateful to her for a task so well accomplished.

The work of preparing the manuscript for publication was made much easier by help of persons at Northern Michigan University. Dr. Jack Rombouts, Vice President for Administrative Affairs, has encouraged the project from the beginning. Maps for the journal were drawn by Mr. Ronald Koshorek of the University's Cartography Section, through the cooperation of Mr. John P. Farrell, Associate Professor of Geography. Mrs. Hazel Cross, Secretary for the Office of Research & Development, an expert typist, prepared the final draft of the entire book. Original illustrations were painstakingly photographed for reproduction by Mr. Charles H. Warner, NMU photographer. Their contributions to the publication of this journal have been substantial.

Through the kindness of Marian H. Brophy, Reference Librarian, New York State Historical Association, Cooperstown, we were able to get some extremely helpful background material on the Penny family, who were early settlers of Putnam County. Also important to our research was material on Penny made available by Agnes H. Tysse, Chief Reference Librarian, University of Michigan Library. Mr. Robert L. Helwig of Marquette loaned us his facsimile copy of the 1837 Detroit city directory which proved to be invaluable as background material in establishing Penny's associations during his life in Detroit. Mr. Lawrence W. Brown, First Assistant of the Burton Historical Collection, Detroit Public Library, and Mrs. Stephen R. Greenberg, Assistant Manuscript Librarian, Chicago Historical Society, aided us in identifying several persons mentioned by Penny. We are also indebted to Mr. Eugene S. Sinervo of Deerton, Michigan, publisher of a local history quarterly, *The Alger Echo,* for his design of the dust jacket.

A real measure of credit for publication of the journal belongs to these people who have generously helped in its preparation. To each we express our gratitude and appreciation.

The Editors

Table of Contents

List of Illustrations

(Unless otherwise noted, illustrations are from the collection of
the John M. Longyear Research Library.)

★   ★   ★   ★

LIST OF MAPS

VIEW OF DETROIT, TAKEN FROM THE CANADA SHORE NEAR THE FERRY, 1836—painted by William James Bennett from a sketch by Frederick Grain. (*Courtesy Burton Historical Collection, Detroit Public Library.*)

Introduction

Michigan was a frontier territory of great promise in the early 1830's when Charles W. Penny left his native New York State for a new life in the rapidly growing territorial capital of Detroit. Vast reaches of virgin country must have had a special attraction for Penny, and he took in stride the adventure and challenge of life on the frontier. His pioneering spirit must have prompted him to eagerly accept Douglass Houghton's invitation to accompany him on his expedition to Lake Superior in 1840, and to return again in 1866.

Penny was born in Putnam County, New York, on January 4, 1812, one of 13 children of Archibald and Henrietta Wilcox Penny. The Pennys were an old colonial family who had moved from Cape Cod, Massachusetts, to Putnam County before the American Revolution.

In 1831 at age 19, Penny went to Detroit and soon was engaged in the dry goods business with Horace Hallock. Here he was very active in civic affairs, helping to establish the Detroit Young Men's Society in 1832, serving as its president in 1835. That year he also was a main force behind the founding of the Detroit Temperance Society. In 1836 he joined the newly-formed Brady Guards, the first uniformed military company west of Buffalo, and saw active duty with the unit on several occasions.

He moved to Jackson in 1841 and opened a dry goods business which he operated for 45 years. Here Penny was a highly respected civic leader and he held several offices in the Episcopal Church.

In order to give his son, Louis, and two daughters, Carrie and Jessica, better educational opportunities, Penny and his wife, Henrietta, moved their family to Ann Arbor in 1886 where they could attend the University of Michigan. Louis died as he was preparing to enter the university; the daughters attended and Jessica eventually taught in the Ishpeming Public Schools.

At the time of his death in Ann Arbor on December 6, 1892, Penny was known and respected throughout the state. In commenting on his long and outstanding career of public service, the *Ann Arbor Register* had this to say: "Among that band of pioneers to whose honesty, industry and intelligence Michigan owes her position today, Mr. Penny has ever been recognized as a peer and a leader."

* * * * *

What prompted Penny to move to Detroit isn't a matter of record. Many young men were establishing new homes in the West, and he was probably heeding a call which had attracted thousands before him and a multitude of others who were to follow. Opening the Erie Canal in 1825 was largely responsible for the western migration and subsequent building of settlements along the shores and waterways of the lower Great Lakes region. These were, in fact, the main avenues of transportation during the 1830's—railroads were yet to be built and there were few good public roads.

Detroit was in the midst of turbulent times when Penny arrived; the city had 6,000 inhabitants and was the capital of the Michigan Territory which had a population of about 60,000. Michigan was seeking statehood and Detroit was alive with rumor, speculation and excitement; politicians from across the territory were gathered in conventions. Steven T. Mason, the "Boy Governor," was proving his worth as a man of exceptional ability. At age 19 he had been appointed Territorial Secretary by President Andrew Jackson, and he had frequently headed the Michigan government as acting governor prior to the death of Governor George B. Porter in 1834. After Governor Porter's death, he became acting governor until he was elected to the office on November 3, 1835, serving until January 7, 1840. Under his leadership, Michigan applied for statehood, and was admitted to the Union on January 26, 1837—but not until a heated boundary controversy with Ohio had been resolved.

When the Michigan Territory was set up in 1805, its southern boundary extended due east from the southern tip of Lake

Michigan to Lake Erie, and residents expected it would remain unchanged when Michigan acquired statehood. However, Ohio had the advantage of being a more populous and influential state; Toledo, which was in the disputed strip, had not only become a Great Lakes port, but the city was the terminus of the Miami Canal. Adherence to the old boundary line would include Toledo in Michigan, and Ohio did not propose to lose such a promising young city. The controversy led to the Toledo War and militia were called out, but the bloodless "war" was settled in Washington with Ohio awarded a ten-mile strip containing Toledo, and Michigan received the western two-thirds of the Upper Peninsula in compensation for its loss.

Another topic of much discussion was the free state-slave state balance which had to be maintained with the admission of new states. When Arkansas, a slave state, was admitted as the 25th state in 1836, the way was open for the free state of Michigan to join the Union the following year.

There is nothing to indicate that Penny took part in political affairs; however, it would have been impossible for any active young man not to have been excited over the prospect of statehood, and he undoubtedly discussed it and other timely issues with his many friends in Detroit.*

It was Penny's privilege to meet and know many of the prominent men of the era, and to be accepted in their circles. In the Detroit Young Mens' Society and the Detroit Temperance Society, he must have been in close contact with the already famous Douglass Houghton. And it is reasonable to assume from later events that they became fairly close friends. They were dedicated Episcopalians. Both apparently sat for portraits by Alvah Bradish at about the same time. As for Penny himself, such information we have could only be found through his activities after his arrival in Detroit. That he was a likable young man of good character, ambitious and willing to work and learn is evidenced in his acceptance by the higher cultural and social elements of the community.

Penny would have read the *Detroit Daily Advertiser* published by George L. Whitney and edited for a time by George Corselius. As an Episcopalian, he would have known Bishop

*Penny was later an abolitionist, and took part in founding the Republican Party at Jackson in 1854.

Samuel A. McCorskry, who was consecrated in 1835 at the age of 33 as the first bishop of the Michigan Diocese. Another cleric of note was the Reverend Bernard O'Cavenagh, rector of Trinity Church. In the political field, he would have known such men as General John R. Williams, elected Detroit's first mayor in 1824 and Levi Cook, a successor, as well as Governor Mason. Others of his acquaintance may have been Charles W. Whipple, speaker of the House of Representatives; Judges Solomon Sibley and George Morrell of the Supreme Court, and Elan Farnsmith, Michigan chancellor. Penny also may have known Henry Schoolcraft, Antoine Beaubien, Seldon McKnight, Major John Biddle, General H. Brady, Francis Palm, Oliver Newberry, Charles C. Trowbridge and a host of other prominent Detroit citizens. We might add to the list Attorneys Alexander Buel, George E. Hand, J. M. Howard and G. Mott Williams. These men not only took an active part in obtaining statehood, but many of them were instrumental in development of Upper Michigan. Some gave their names to streets in Detroit as well as to towns in the northern peninsula.

Until the 1840's, little was known of the interior of the Upper Peninsula. Pierre Esprit Radisson, Jacques Marquette, Claude Allouez, Louis Jolliet and other French missionaries and explorers had skirted the shores of Lake Superior almost 200 years earlier. Radisson arrived in 1658 and Marquette travelled through the area a decade later. During the Jesuit priest's three-year stay, mostly spent in the Chequamegon Bay area, he prepared what was to become one of the most famous base maps of the Lake Superior country, which was published in Paris in 1672. Voyageurs, coureurs de bois and fur traders seldom ventured far from the waterways making their camps, as did the Indians, on the lake shore or on banks of streams. As they travelled in birch bark canoes, clinging closely to the shore, they carried provisions westward and peltries east, and gave little thought to the mysterious hills which rose above the lake at many points along its coasts. Governor Lewis Cass on his expedition through the Lake Superior region in 1820, Henry Schoolcraft in his several journeys in the 1830's, and others, never ventured very far inland.

Many of the early explorers found small lumps of float copper—pieces which had been sheared from larger masses by glacial action—but the extent of deposits were not realized until Douglass Houghton made his discoveries in the 1830's and early 1840's. Even then a true valuation of the copper wealth remained unknown, not to be fully exposed until after his untimely death in October, 1845.

Early interior exploration of the Upper Peninsula was made by William Austin Burt, Deputy United States Surveyor, and his party in the early 1840's, which resulted in discovery of iron ore on the Marquette Range in September, 1844. It was during the decades of the 1840's and 1850's that Michigan began to realize the loss of the Toledo Strip had its compensations in the enormous mineral deposits being discovered in the Upper Peninsula. During the 1850's and the next several decades, mine after mine was opened for both copper and iron ores. Ship loads of minerals moved to the lower lake ports from Marquette, the Keweenaw Peninsula and Ontonagon. The pace was accelerated with the opening of the Saint Marys Falls Ship Canal in June of 1855. The wounded pride of the young state over the loss of Toledo was soon replaced with a great wave of speculation in the famed Copper Country. Thus, the first mineral rush in the United States began soon after Penny's trip to Lake Superior with Douglass Houghton.

* * *

Houghton's expeditions played a key part in unlocking the riches of the Keweenaw Peninsula for Michigan and the nation. His discoveries had been made only after years of exhausting surveys in the state's most rugged regions. Michigan was anxious to gain factual knowledge of mineral wealth which up to then had been only suspected. More accurate charts of its many miles of watercourses and better knowledge of the flora and fauna were also major goals of his surveys.

In 1837 and 1838, there was a reorganization of the State Geological Survey to include mineralogical, geological, zoological and botanical aspects of the state. A $12,000 annual appropriation was to be made for the years 1838-1841, totaling approximately $36,000, to finance the survey. A final survey report was to be given to the State Legislature no later than March 1, 1841.

Although the official scope of the three-year survey was to cover a wide number of subjects, its immediate aims were some-

DOUGLASS HOUGHTON, GEOLOGIST, LAKE SUPERIOR—*from* Memoir of Douglass Houghton *by Alvah Bradish, after an original portrait by Mr. Bradish.*

what more limited. Of primary concern was a mineralogical and geological survey of the Upper Peninsula—especially areas believed to contain copper ores. Another important objective was to develop salt works from wells at various points in the Grand and Tittabawassee River areas. The survey was also to study the state's watercourses, its rivers, harbors and Great Lakes shore areas.

Houghton was appointed to head the reorganized survey. Although the state was in virtual bankruptcy following the Panic of 1837—brought on by wild speculation in canal and railroad ventures, and the failure of many "wildcat" banks—money was made available for the survey as it was considered of prime importance.

Michigan as a state was only a year old in 1838, and it now had a population of 174,000. Detroit, the capital, had grown to slightly over 8,000 residents. Upper Michigan had only two political divisions, Mackinac County with 664 persons, and Chippewa, having a population of 366—giving the entire Upper Peninsula a population of just over 1,000! Its settlements could be counted on the fingers of one hand. They were Mackinac Island, the largest settlement with about 500 residents, and St. Ignace, Sault Ste. Marie and L'Anse. The remaining area was a vast wilderness with an Indian population not much larger than that of white men.

During the first year of the survey, 1838, Houghton spent most of his time organizing and directing development of the salt springs and wells. He took a trip along the Lake Michigan and Huron shores of the Lower Peninsula, made notes on the soils of these shore areas, and explored the lower parts of the major rivers.

In 1839, he placed deputies in charge of the salt works, and he spent three months, from June into September, in the Upper Peninsula. During this time, he explored the Lake Michigan shore from St. Ignace to the Menominee River, and also the shore area from St. Ignace to Sault Ste. Marie. On this trip he made special notes on the soils, timber reserves and supply of commercial-type fish. Aware of the need for a canal at Sault Ste. Marie—especially if valuable mineral deposits were discovered in the Lake Superior district—Houghton made an extensive survey of a canal site and all aspects of such a project. He concluded his work in the field by examining mineral deposits in Branch County.

The climax of the survey really came with the exploration of the south shore of Lake Superior and the copper-bearing areas of the Keweenaw Peninsula during the spring and summer of 1840. His estimate of the extent of the copper range was amazingly accurate, as proven by subsequent development. Although Penny and most of the expedition returned to Lower Michigan at the end of the summer, Houghton remained to make explorations deeper into the interior of the copper region and other areas along the south shore of Lake Superior. He made detailed surveys of the area between the Montreal and Ontonagon Rivers, which was in dispute, being claimed by both Michigan and the Wisconsin Territory. Houghton was anxious that the area be retained by Michigan as he thought it might contain valuable mineral resources.

Upon return to Detroit, he successfully persuaded the Legislature to extend the March 1, 1841 deadline for his report. He also made rapid progress on an extensive mapping project of survey areas throughout the state.

One of Houghton's most rewarding achievements was the settlement in 1841 of the boundary controversy with Wisconsin, in which he played a major role. Michigan was allowed to retain its entire claim to lands east of the Montreal River. Houghton spent several months surveying in the Chocolay River area in the central Upper Peninsula, the iron range to the west and south, and areas east of the Chocolay. He was aided throughout the survey by William A. Burt. However, rheumatism and general fatigue plagued Houghton during the summer of 1841.

In 1842, he did little field work, concentrating on catching up on mounting paperwork, his final report, and a series of county maps he was publishing as part of the state survey. The year 1843 was spent in a similar manner. His preliminary reports, cautiously worded, already were stirring widespread interest in the copper deposits of the Keweenaw region.

Money was still extremely tight in Michigan in 1844, a situation which prompted Houghton to convince Federal officials that the U. S. Linear and Michigan Geological Survey efforts should be combined—at a considerable savings to both governments. He was particularly anxious that such combined efforts should produce the finest possible map of the Upper Peninsula.

Houghton's work was receiving high praise throughout the state and from many points in the country. Personally, his esteem was even greater. It should be noted that when state funds ran short, Houghton sometimes used his own money to complete a particular phase of a project, such was his dedication to the survey.

Ill health still hampered Houghton's efforts in 1845, but, nevertheless, with the aid of Burt, a very successful season was completed in the survey of the Upper Peninsula mineral region. Houghton had virtually all his notes complete for his final report and maps, which were being eagerly awaited not only by persons in Michigan, but investors in the East interested in exploiting copper reserves in the Upper Peninsula.

Thousands were shocked when, on the evening of October 13, 1845, Houghton and several companions were drowned as their small craft overturned and was swamped in a sudden squall near Eagle River on the western shores of the Keweenaw Peninsula.

Houghton's notes were never compiled into his final report, and in the years following his death, most of his notes were lost. The $32,800 actually expended by the Legislature never brought the return on the investment originally anticipated. Some of Houghton's material on the Upper Peninsula surveys was published jointly by Burt and Bela Hubbard, who had been Houghton's assistant, and others renewed some of the survey efforts. The cooperative U. S.-state survey was carried on for a few years, then discontinued.

Although what would have been his greatest contribution was never realized, Houghton left an indelible mark on early Michigan and his work was largely responsible for the birth of the mining industry in the Upper Peninsula.

Penny's journal of the 1840 trip to Lake Superior adds a valuable new perspective to an expedition which holds a prominent place in Michigan history.

JAMES L. CARTER AND ERNEST H. RANKIN

Marquette, Michigan
September 4, 1969

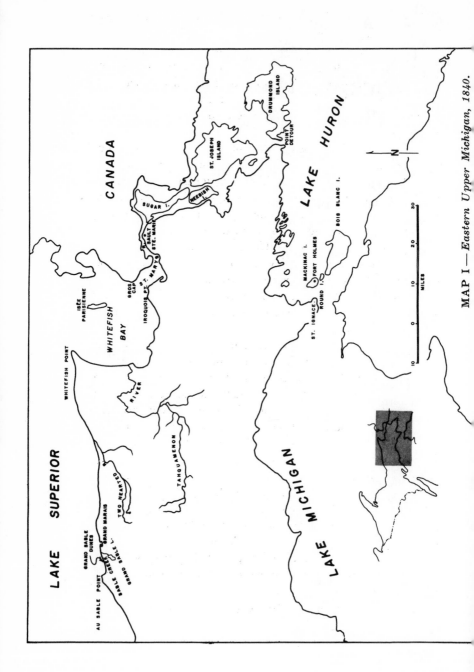

MAP I — *Eastern Upper Michigan, 1840.*

Mackinac and the Sault
—The Northern Frontier

I left Detroit, on the Steamboat *Illinois,* Thursday, May 21st, 1840, and arrived at Mackinaw [Island] Friday evening. Distance 320 miles.

Saturday, May 23rd.

I started this morning, with Messrs. B.[1] & F.[2] Hubbard and Tealson[3] for a ramble on the island. We first visited Robinson's folly,[4] a high point of rock over-hanging the water at the South East angle of the island. On this point, Robinson once commander of the fort, built a summer house where he gave dinner parties and champagne frolics almost daily. One night a portion of the rock, summer house and all, fell into the lake, hence its name. About 100 rods, almost due north from the Folly, is the celebrated arched rock. It rises almost perpendicular from the water to a height of about 200 feet. The base of the arch is 30 feet in width—the height is 50 feet; this we ascertained by measurement. The stone of which it is composed, is full of seams and cracks, so much so that small pieces are frequently

---

[1]Bela Hubbard (1814-1896), was first assistant to Douglass Houghton, and was a geologist and surveyor. He arrived in Wayne County, Mich., from New York State in 1835. See an account of the 1840 Lake Superior expedition in his *Memorials of a Half-Century* (New York: G. P. Putnam's Sons), 1887.

[2]Frederick Hubbard was a special assistant in charge of instrumental observations.

[3]H. Tealson (Thielson), a civil engineer, was a supernumerary as was Charles Penny.

[4]Robinson's Folly (originally Robertson's) is the most prominent bluff on Mackinac Island, named for Capt. Daniel Robertson, a British commandant of the island from 1782 to 1787. Another version of the story is that he fell in love with a beautiful Indian maiden, daughter of a chief. Although the chief had promised her to a brave, whom she didn't love, she and Robertson were secretly married and lived in a cottage high on the bluff. The disgruntled brave eventually discovered the pair and stabbed Robertson's wife to death. He and Robertson fell from the bluff during the ensuing scuffle, and both were killed on the rocks at the lake shore below.

1

MACKINAC, VIEW OF FORT AND TOWN—from Picturesque America, edited by William Cullen Bryant, Demumb

falling off; and I have no doubt that the tooth of time would completely destroy the arch in less than a century. We then visited pyramid rock [Sugar Loaf]. This is an isolated rock, near the centre of the island, having a base of about 30 feet in diameter and rising, as near as we could judge by the eye, 150 feet. Fort Holmes stands upon the highest point of land on the island. The island is in general 150 feet high. The little hill on which Fort Holmes[5] is built is very steep and the walls of the fort are 318 feet above the level of the lake. A little South West from the Fort is Skull Rock, so called from a quantity of human skulls having been found in a cave which penetrates its base. The Indians have various traditions respecting these skulls. One is that a party of braves being hotly pursued by their enemies sought refuge within the cave, and were followed with so much ardour by their pursuers, that being tightly wedged in, both friends and foes perished by suffocation. The skulls were found there by the traveler, Henry,[6] who being here at the time of the massacre at old Fort Mackinaw, was secreted in this cave for safety by a friendly Indian. The view from Fort Holmes is truly beautiful. To the North lies the main land, distant 6 or 7 miles—to the East you look out on Lake Huron, Southeast, lies Bois Blanc island, about 10 miles long. South is Round island, separated from Mackinaw by the primal strait for navigation, about 1 mile wide. Look west and you see islands, and the north and south shore, stretching away to the entrance of Lake Michigan. All around you is a beautiful sheet of water; under your feet, as it were, is the village of Mackinaw overlooked by the fort with its walls and pickets and block houses neatly whitewashed.

Sunday, May 24th.

This has been a beautiful, sunshiny day, with scarce a breeze

---

[5]Fort Holmes was originally called Fort George by the British (for King George III) who built it when they captured the island during the War of 1812. It was taken over by the Americans after the war and renamed Fort Holmes after Maj. Andrew H. Holmes, who was killed in the Battle of Mackinac Island, Aug. 4, 1814.

[6]Alexander Henry (1739-1824), carried on a fur trade between Albany, N. Y., Mackinac and points west. During the Pontiac Conspiracy in the early 1760's, he was hidden by friendly Indians in Skull Rock. After returning to the East in 1776. he wrote his famous *Travels and Adventures of Alexander Henry.*

to ruffle the waters. After breakfast Gen. Williams,[7] Lieut. Pemberton,[8] T. C. Emons[9] and myself took a stroll—went to the arched rock and three of us crossed the arch. This is no great feat, the soiling and tearing of clothes being quite a sufficient offset to the glory of the deed. We returned, went to the Presbyterian church, or rather meeting—held in the new courthouse. Attendance very small, though as large in proportion to the number of inhabitants, as attend church in Detroit, on a pleasant Sunday. The remainder of the day, spent in reading, talking & lounging, has left me with the impression that they have very long days in Mackinaw.

Monday, May 25th.

Still no conveyance to the Sault Ste. Marie, & I begin to tire of this place. All day we have had a cold East wind, and just the very fog that occasions so many suicides in England. Last evening the *Great Western* was here on her way to Chicago; and this morning the *New England,* bound for Buffalo. But I have one thing to comfort me—that is good-living. Mrs. Lasley [10] furnishes an excellent table—corn soup, whitefish, &c., are among the luxuries of the island. I have already eaten so many whitefish, that my tail wiggles as I go along the street.

I forgot to mention yesterday, my visit to the lover's leap— a high perpendicular point about mid-way of the southern shore of the island. It is one of the handsomest spots on the island— being crowned with two fine pine trees for a shade—and affords the best view of the islands and bays and straits that can be obtained at any one point. Hope for a boat tomorrow.

Tuesday, May 26th.

East wind & fog! Are we to be kept here a week? Dr. Houghton and his party put off this morning for Drummond's Island. They will have a hard pull, unless the wind abates. We have partly engaged a little dumpling of a schooner, called the *Rodoph,* to take us up, but the weather is

---

[7]Gen. Thomas Williams (1815-1862) was the son of John R. Williams, the first mayor of Detroit. He was killed in the Battle of Baton Rouge (La.) during the Civil War.

[8]J. C Pemberton was a second lieutenant in the 4th Artillery.

[9]T. C. Emons is unidentifiable.

[10]Mrs. Lasley was presumably the wife of George Lasley, a fur trader.

ROBINSON'S FOLLY—*from* Picturesque America, *edited by William Cullen Bryant. Drawn by J. Douglas Woodward.*

unfavorable for leaving port. I had written thus far, when I took a walk & heard the Steamboat *Fair Port* coming in. She arrived about 10 o'clock, but we could not prevail upon her to go to the Sault. Lieut. Root[11] with eighteen soldiers chartered the *Rodoph* and put out. Mr. Bushnell,[12] Indian Agent at La Point, and myself engaged some voyageurs to take us up in a small Mackinaw boat. About 7 o'clock P.M. the wind died away & we started. We had a traverse of 12 miles to make which is as bad as the open lake,—this, too, in the night, in a small open boat over rough swells. As we started out I could not but admire the intrepidity of these hardy men—thus trusting themselves, without light or compass in so frail a bark, to the mercy of a treacherous lake. For myself I was too much delighted and exhilarated by the graceful motions of the boat and the novelty of the situation, to heed the danger. The night proved somewhat foggy, and we were more than two hours out of sight of land. About 12 o'clock we got on shore—built a fire and lay down to sleep in the open air. I was too cold to sleep much—to say nothing of the inconvenience of laying on a bed of round stones.

Wednesday, May 27th.

As soon as day-light had fairly appeared (and that was ½ past 3) our men were up and put our baggage into the boat; and then roused Mr. Bushnell & myself. The sun rose clear and bright. Not a cloud obscured the sky and not a breeze ruffled the lake. Our men bent themselves to their oars—and seemed to heed the labor as little as a steam engine. But Mr. Bushnell & myself were almost killed with the heat; there was no escape from the scorching sun. We were literally *fried*. But the moment the sun went down, the air became cold—so much that a heavy over coat & a thick blanket wrapped around us, could hardly make us comfortable. We reached the "Sailor's Encampment" about 9 o'clock, and after eating a hearty supper of cold pork & bread, lay down to rest. I slept pretty well—having grass instead of stones for a bed. We traveled to-day near 60 miles.

---

[11]Lieut William Root was an assistant quartermaster at Fort Brady.

[12]Daniel P. Bushnell was appointed Indian agent at La Pointe on March 18, 1837.

Thursday, May 28th.

This morning at daylight we were again on the way, and arrived at the Sault Ste. Marie, about 10 o'clock A. M.—having traveled 90 miles in a day and a half. I was quite pleased with the scenery of the river. It is very broad—perhaps averaging 5 miles and filled with islands—so thick that for most of the way we could see the mainland on neither side. The river, at the falls, runs a little to the south of east—is about half a mile in width, and the rapids extend up and down about ¼ of a mile—where the water dashes, and foams and roars, and almost equals Niagara in noise. I have quite a severe headache, and shall defer my letter writing and so on till to-morrow.

Friday, May 29th.

My principal business to-day has been writing two letters— one to my sister Louisa and one to Mr. Wickware[13] of Detroit. Dr. Houghton came up this morning about 3 o'clock from Drummond's Island, with one of his boats, and took it over the portage. His other boat is expected sometime to-morrow. Went up to see the vessel belonging to the Cleveland Co., or Northern Lake Co. as they style themselves. She is a very snug, handsome schooner, and was taken over without receiving the slightest injury. Became acquainted with Mr. Mendonhall, [14] one of the owners who had charge of the business last winter. He was one of four who took the vessel over. The vessel is now loaded, and they intend sailing to-morrow for La Point, where it is their intention to build a store, warehouse and wharf, and compete with the American Fur Co. on their own ground. A half-breed, named Ashiel Cadot,[15] a fine, intelligent man well acquainted with the Indians, and with the Lake trade, is to accompany Mr. Mendonhall, and I have no doubt of the complete success of their experiment.

---

[13]Penny was probably referring to Cornelius Wickware who was in partnership with F. Eldred. The firm of Eldred & Wickware was listed in the 1837 *Directory of the City of Detroit* as "Hardware and Commission Merchants," located at 186 Jefferson Ave.

[14]Cyrus Mendonhall, a New York investor, also had mining and shipping interests.

[15]Ashiel Cadot, more likely Cadotte, is believed to have been a fur trader and interpreter. The name was long established in the Lake Superior fur trade.

7

Saturday, May 30th.

Last evening we had a most splendid display of Northern lights. At 10 o'clock the whole heavens appeared to be in a blaze—streaks of light flashed up toward the zenith from every part of the horizon, and we could read a newspaper very well. It exceeded in brilliancy anything of that kind I had ever seen. About 9 this morning the remainder of Houghton's party came up. We called on the commanding officer of the fort [Brady], Capt. Johnson,[16] and Mr. Ord,[17] the Indian Agent. In the afternoon we made arrangement with Mr. Ashman,[18] for a larger boat in place of one of the Doctor's. Mr. Tealson & myself got into it and were pushed up the falls by six good, strong natives, and had the pleasure of descending the falls in the same manner. The ride down the falls is rather exciting to a yankee. The water boils & foams around the boat which shoots along like an arrow—while through the clear water you see the eternal rocks lifting their heads as if to dash you in pieces. As we were starting from the head of the Millrace for the purpose of descending, the Indian who stood in the bow for the purpose of directing the course to be steered, asked very earnestly for tobacco. Supposing he wished a good quid, I handed him a small plug, which, instead of putting into his mouth, he laid carefully upon the end of a log which reaches out into the lake, as an offering to the Great Spirit of the Falls, saying, as he did so, that we should now have a safe passage down. In the evening we called on Mr. Bingham[19] and family at the mission. He is a very fine, pleasant man, and has an amiable daughter, who was married to Mr. Hulbert[20] last fall. On the whole, I feel better pleased with the Sault, than with Mackinaw. The

---

[16]Capt. Johnson—apparently Seth Johnson who previously served at Fort Dearborn (Chicago).

[17]James Ord arrived at Sault Ste. Marie in July of 1838, as sub-Indian agent, and became agent succeeding Henry R. Schoolcraft, serving there until 1850. See *Michigan History Magazine*, Vol. 31 (Sept., 1947), pp. 344-345.

[18]Samuel Ashmun was a fur trader and interpreter, and an employee of the American Fur Co. at various posts in the Northwest. He arrived at Sault Ste. Marie in 1824, where he became a prominent citizen.

[19]Rev. Abel Bingham (1786-1865) came to Sault Ste. Marie in 1828 and built a Baptist mission school there in 1829.

[20]John Hulbert was a sutler at the Fort Brady garrison. He and Marie Schoolcraft Hulbert were parents of Edwin James Hulbert, a famous geologist.

ARCHED ROCK, MACKINAC—*from* Picturesque America, *edited by William Cullen Bryant. Drawn by J. Douglas Woodward.*

scenery here is equally interesting, and the inhabitants more in-
dustrious. About a mile above this point, there will one day be
a city larger than Detroit. It is a pity to see such a splendid
water power perfectly useless. It is valueless as there is no timber in the country and grain cannot be raised to advantage.

Sunday, May 31st.

Attended Church this morning at the Mission house, and
heard a very good, plain sermon from the Rev. Mr. Bingham.
This evening he preached to the natives—through an interpreter.
There are about twenty lodges of the Indians here at present,
who subsist chiefly by fishing. The whitefish are very large
and fine, and go currently for six pence, in trade. In the afternoon I wrote to Mr. Hartshorn. This is probably the last letter
I shall write for two months. The weather continues very fine,
and dry. There has been no rain here, I am told, for six weeks
—none of any consequence since last fall. In the winter there
was about three feet of snow, which, in melting, supplied in
some measure the want of rain. The water in Lake Superior
is reported by Capt. Stanard[21] to be three feet lower than it was
last year. It has fallen in Lake Huron, but not more than half
as much. We intend starting to-morrow with our largest boat,
and Doctor Houghton will follow us about Thursday.

---

[21]Charles C. Stanard was master of the 112-ton schooner *John Jacob
Astor*, a fur trading vessel built by the American Fur Co., and launched
on Lake Superior at Sault Ste. Marie during the first week of August,
1835. Benjamin Stanard became captain of the *Astor* at the beginning
of the 1843 season, and remained in that capacity until the vessel was
wrecked near the Keweenaw Peninsula on Sept. 21, 1844.

Whitefish Bay to Grand Marais

Monday, June 1st.

Last night about 12 we had a very heavy thunder storm of rain and hail, and the weather has been cloudy all day with an east wind. We began preparation for starting quite early, but were unable to get away till ½ past six in the afternoon. Our boat was loaded with about thirteen barrels, bulk & tents & baggage besides. On board are Messrs. C. C. Douglass,[22] B. Hubbard, F. Hubbard and myself. The wind being favorable· we ran up to a bay, about a mile East of Gros Cap and encamped at 10 o'clock. We had much difficulty in making shore as the water is very shallow for ½ mile out and we ran aground often. When within 15 or 20 rods of the beach we struck fast, and our four voyageurs took us on their backs and set us safely on dry land. In like manner they brought to shore all our luggage & a large portion of the boat's load. This bay is about 13 miles from Sault Ste. Marie.

Tuesday, June 2nd.

This morning early we moved from our encampment, conceiving it to be a dangerous place in case of a South or West wind. We started for Gros Cap—ran aground repeatedly but finally made the shore some ½ mile above our starting point. It began to rain as soon as we had got on shore and pitched our tents. In the forest here I notice maple, birch, mountain ash, pine, spruce & cedar. I should have said that we are located on Victoria's land—and very good land it is too. I stated last night that we were encamped about a mile from Gros Cap. This shows how easily the eye may be deceived. In walking it this morning we set it down as three. Although it has rained all

---

[22]Columbus C. Douglass was an assistant geologist and a pioneer of Houghton, Mich. He was a cousin of Douglass Houghton.

day we have moved about some. We went to Gros Cap in the forenoon. It is quite a cliff—towering to a height of six hundred & twenty feet. It rises almost perpendicularly from the lake and is composed chiefly of a reddish, hard rock—destitute of all fossil remains. On the opposite side is Point Iroquois, of about equal height. These two pillars form as it were a magnificent door, or gateway into the great lake. Point Iroquois is so named in commemoration of the terrible slaughter of near three thousand warriors of that tribe by the Chippewas. They were the masters, as well as enemies of the Chippewas, and being encamped on that point, sung their war song & danced their war dance in fancied security until completely exhausted, when a band of Chippewas appeared in their camp & cut them to pieces.

Mr. Douglass killed six pigeons & four plover[23] this morning, which will sweeten our pork. The eastern storm still continues & we keep our encampment for the night. I was vexed in the extreme to think I should be so careless as to leave my fishing tackle—designed for brook trout—at the Sault. We have everything else to make us comfortable—plenty of provisions—tea, sugar, butter, brandy, tobacco, pipes and many other of the comforts of life. The cossett & traveling case furnished by Mr. Ashman—are just the things to make us comfortable. He had been in these regions before us.

Wednesday, June 3rd.

Rain and fog have continued with little intermission all day. We crossed over to Point Iroquois, a distance of about six miles, early in the morning and took breakfast. We ascended the point but our view was completely obscured by the dense fog. The lake is very shallow till you get a mile from the shore. In truth we grounded several times, when more than that distance from the shore, in a foot of water. The bottom is perfectly level, and resembles a vast pavement of round stones from three to twelve inches in diameter. We dined on a beautiful bank, covered with the Norway pine for miles along the coast, and our dinner consisted of pork roasted on the end of a stick and

---

[23]Plover are shore-inhabiting birds, sometimes called killdeer.

12

hardbread. While at dinner, two Indian canoes passed us going east. About fifteen miles from Iroquois, we found white sandstone. We encamped about sunset at the mouth of Tequimiminen [Tahquamenon] River. There we found a Chippewa village of a dozen lodges—the first real Indian village I ever saw. I was equally surprised & pleased on entering their lodges to find them so neat, comfortable and well provided. The chief, a fine looking man about 35 years of age, came to our boat as soon as we landed, leading three of his little boys—smart looking fellows & nearly of the same size. We then visited the lodges of the tribe, saw the chief's four wives, and found everybody comfortable. I have never yet lived in a place where there are not many poor families in a much more destitute and wretched condition than these poor Indians. In one lodge we got some sugar—very white & clean.

Thursday, June 4th.

Early in the morning we left our encampment and proceeded up the river. It was cold and foggy, and we were almost frozen to death. At 8 o'clock we stopped and cooked breakfast, and while eating, the sun appeared—a truly welcome sight—and the remainder of the day was beautiful. Having proceeded about fifteen miles, we came to a rapid, where we dined, made an unsuccessful attempt to catch trout and at 3 o'clock started on our return back. From the rapids the mouth of the river bears East-Southeast, but in its windings turns to almost every point of the compass. Its average width is about three hundred feet—varying in depth from 15 to 30 feet. Its current is very sluggish—almost imperceptible—and its banks generally high. and covered with a thick, heavy growth of Norway pine, birch, maple, hemlock, spruce and balsam fir. There are a few fine trees of white pine on both sides of the river, but not enough to render the country valuable for lumber. The weather, the river and the banks were all beautiful, our seats in the boat comfortable, and all things seem to conspire to render this a happy day. What could trouble us? Care we had left behind in the regions of civilization, where it properly belongs. Our wants are amply provided for, for at least three months to come; and we have four good men to tote us along, pitch our tents, build

SAULT STE. MARIE FROM THE AMERICAN SIDE—*from* The Great Lakes or Inland Seas of America, *compiled by J. Disturnell.*

fires, cook our victuals, sing songs and talk French & Indian. For, be it known these unlettered half-breeds speak three languages fluently. We reached the rapids a little before two o'clock, took our luncheon and examined the surrounding country, but found nothing of interest. After an unsuccessful attempt at fishing, we turned our course for the lake; but, night coming on, we encamped on the bank of the river, about five miles from its mouth. The bank here spreads off into a fine elevated plain, covered with Norway pine and reindeer moss. The country on both sides of the river is thickly wooded—some of the trees being of a great height—with birch, white & pitch pine, hemlock, spruce & maple. Here I saw some of the handsomest and largest balsam firs I had ever seen. We estimated their height at over 100 feet. What would some of our city folks give for a few of them to adorn their pleasure grounds?

Friday, June 5th.

This morning early we ran down to the lake, stopped at the Indian village and bought some sugar & a paddle; and finding the wind favorable, hoisted sail and stood for White Fish Point, distant about 20 miles, where we arrived at 11 o'clock. The point is rather low, with a fine gravelly beach about four rods in width; then comes sand, which is moved about by the winds, forming hills twenty to thirty feet high, and is scantily covered with small scrub pine. There are seven or eight wigwams on the point occupied by fisherman and Indians. The whitefish usually appear there in abundance by the 20th of May, yet, but few have been taken this spring. Having satisfied our curiosity and refreshed ourselves with a cup of tea, we again moved forward—the coast bearing West-Southwest. The wind had died away, and our men put on their towing line and harnessed themselves into it, and we moved off in real canal style—the beach forming one of the best tow paths imaginable. About six miles from the point we found a party of fishermen recently located, and fitted out by the Northern Lake Company. They have a fine seine, but are unable to use it at present for want of lead to sink it. The leader of the party fished on the same ground last season and says he could have put up a thousand barrels with one seine, if he had been supplied with salt and barrels. Soon after leaving them it began to rain gently, and we encamped on the beach [near Crisp Point], about twelve miles from the point. The beach is very wide and fine from the point to this place, and the same as far as the eye can extend west. Every quarter of a mile would make a first rate fishing ground. About fifty yards from the shore is the first sand bank, about the same distance farther inland lies another, and so on in succession lie four sand ridges varying in height from 10 to 40 feet. Between these ridges the ground is low—often covered with water and a scanty growth of timber.

Saturday, June 6th.

It rained hard all night and all the forenoon. Before daylight the wind began to blow strong from the Northwest, and when we got up the lake was white with foam. After moving our tents back of the third sand ridge and drawing our boat farther up on the beach, we stood for a long time exposed to the pitiless pelting of the furious storm, for the purpose of witnessing a scene, to me, so new and grand. The swells were regular and high and broke on the outer bar with that deep thundering roar, which is heard as you stand under the falls of Niagara. In the afternoon the storm ceased and we amused ourselves by measuring the height of trees. One old white pine, about ten rods from our tents, measured one hundred & forty-four 5/10 feet. The day has been very cold for the season of the year. Thermometer in the morning stood at 42°—noon 46° —evening 40°. Should the wind continue we may be weather bound here for several days, for it would be impossible to put out through these breakers.

Sunday, June 7th.

The air this morning was calm, and the sun shone out clear and bright. For a luxury we had slapjacks for breakfast. These are made of flour and water only, and with butter and sugar make a first rate dish. In the forenoon Douglass and myself took a stroll back in the woods, and were nearly eaten up by mosquitoes. We found the land undulating and very thickly covered with trees. It might almost be termed as impenetrable forest. Most of the trees appear to be young; while here and there stands a venerable pine, or hemlock of enormous height and size, their former companions lie strewed on the ground. It would seem as though the forest trees, at long intervals, grew old and decayed, and were succeeded by an entirely new growth. At two o'clock the waves had so far subsided that we were enabled to launch our boat and put to sea. We ran as far as Twin [Two-hearted] River, when—a head wind arriving—we were obliged to run in for shelter & encamped for the night. The river is very rapid near its mouth—so much so that it was difficult to enter it. For about half a mile before entering the lake it runs parallel with the lake, and is separated from it by a strip of gravel, not more than two rods wide, which looks almost precisely like a long pier. Here we caught twenty fine speckled brook trout, which were served up for dinner at seven o'clock. I would here remark that we usually dine about 7, that being a fashionable hour in this country. In such vulgar places as London and Paris, they dine an hour or two earlier. These trout are the finest fish to catch or eat that I have ever seen. They are quite free of bones.

Monday, June 8th.

A little after sunrise (which rises at 4 o'clock) we were on our way, with a pretty stiff wind off shore. At eight o'clock we stopped for breakfast. While it was preparing I wandered along the beach and picked up a very pretty agate. We had looked for these stones a great deal, but had found only one before, which was picked up yesterday by Mr. Douglass. We arrived at Grand Marais River at 3 o'clock this afternoon and here we are to remain until the arrival of Doctor Houghton. At the mouth of the river is one of the prettiest bays I have yet seen on the lakes, and is a perfectly safe harbor for schooners in any wind. It would measure about three-fourths of a mile by a mile and a quarter. We are now 45 miles from White Fish Point—90 miles from the Sault Ste. Mary's. Immediately after landing we began our trout fishing without taking one—the water is too sluggish. We have just fastened nine large hooks to a long cord and anchored them out in the bay for the purpose of catching some salmon trout. One soon gets fish hungry on hardbread.

Grand Sables and Pictured Rocks

Tuesday, June 9th.

Not a fish on our hooks this morning, and, what is worse, we spent all the forenoon trying to catch them without success. We went up the river as far as our boat would float, and found it a very poor affair. It is a small stream, not over a foot & a half deep on an average, destitute of fish, and surrounded by a tamarac swamp. In the afternoon we took a walk to the Grand Sable, on the beach. The sand beach, around the bay which forms the harbor here, is the handsomest I ever saw. A brisk walk of an hour and a half brought us to the sand hills. As we approach them, the air is filled with moving sand. A small, rapid stream [Sable Creek] separates them from the timbered land on the east. This stream looks muddy, being constantly filled with the flying sand which it carries to the lake. It is the outlet of a beautiful little lake [Grand Sable Lake], about two miles back of the shore. The sand hills are bounded on the east by this outlet, and extend almost to the little lake. They extend along the coast of Superior about three miles. Of their height I will give no opinion; as we intend (weather permitting and the Doctor not coming) to visit them again tomorrow and take along instruments to measure them. The top is a vast, undulating plain of moving sand, looking perhaps much like a desert. The wind packs the sand so hard that it is quite good walking over them. The wind blowing for a long time in one direction moves so large a body of sand as to cover up the adjoining trees, and we saw the tops of some tall cedars just peeping through the sand. The sand is mostly very fine and handsome, at a few points it is mixed with gravel and round stone, which have evidently been once subject to the action of the waves, but which now lie snugly imbedded at a height of 3 & 4 hundred feet. In walking over these gravelly spots we picked up several agates. The sides of these hills are as steep as sand can be made to lie, and we all descended by sliding down on the seat of honor. The scene is magnificent beyond my power of description. In fact, I do not think a description or drawing could convey any just idea of it, though executed by the hand of a master. We must look at it again to-morrow. The mosquitoes, although not very numerous, are very troublesome to me. Their bite is so poisonous as to cause the flesh to swell and burn for several days, and finally to become a running sore. This has been the case with my face. One bit me last night under the left eye, and I am now almost blind. With the exception of such little annoyances I enjoy my trip greatly. I have a most voracious appetite, and am growing quite fat & tough. I can sleep under my tent without taking cold, and bear a good deal of hardship without fatigue. Six hours sleep is all we allow ourselves and that takes all the night, and something more. If the Doctor doesn't come by to-morrow night we intend to run back to Twin River, where we can luxuriate on the little speckled trout. There is no kind of game in this neighborhood—not even bears. We have not seen a pigeon these five days, nor are the woods here enlivened with the song of birds as they are at this season of the year in more temperate climates.

Wednesday, June 10th.

This morning we repaired to the "Grand Sable," or great sand hills, and I found abundant occasion to regret that I had never learned the art of sketching. I rambled over them for more than four hours, and could have spent the day there with great pleasure. I descended from the highest and steepest point to the lake—rather sliding than walking—and attempted to make a sketch of it. It is as rude as a first attempt might be supposed to be, and yet I think it bears some resemblence to nature. Our men went back to the small lake I spoke of yesterday, and returned with their handkerchiefs filled with *snow* which they found in large quantities buried under the sand. Everything about these sand hills is curious. Why should they remain in such lofty heights, when the winds are constantly sweeping their substance into the valleys and lake, and why should so many spots on them look precisely like the present beach of the lake? Did the waters once rise to such a height? And then, the stones found there show plainly the long continued action of water, and the effects of most intense heat. It is not my province to offer any speculations as to the causes of these appearances.

On our return we reached camp just in time to escape a thunder shower, that confined us to our tents till five o'clock. About this time Capt. Johnson arrived from the Sault Ste. Mary's —bringing me a letter from Mr. Ashmun, and intelligence that the Doctor is weather bound on Parisian Island [Isle Parisienne] —about 12 miles east of White Fish Point. It is, of course, entirely uncertain when we shall see him. The more I see of this little bay the better I like it. The water in it is very deep, and perfectly calm—no matter which way the wind may come.

The bar at the entrance of the bay is sufficient to spoil it for a harbor. The bar is broad, and the water on an average not more then 6 feet. It is 10 feet in one spot only, and that could not be passed in a storm.

Thursday, June 11th.

We had a feast to-day. In the morning slapjacks & sugar— our dinner table has all the delicacies of the forest—wild duck, pigeon, partridge, squirrel, &c. Mr. Douglass, as yet, has been the only successful hunter. I ventured into the woods once, but the mosquitoes made game of me. Their bite is so poisonous that my flesh becomes swollen & inflamed, and large sores are formed over my face, neck & hands. In the forenoon I assisted Mr. F. Hubbard in sounding and triangulating the bay. In the afternoon we trolled for large trout and caught—nothing. About 4 o'clock the Doctor came up and relieved us of all further anxiety as to what we should do with ourselves. The truth is, four days is too long to stay in one place. But we have been three times to the Grand Sable, the only place of interest in our vicinity, and that is ever new. A walk over the top of it which is about 2 miles by 4, must give one a very correct idea of the great African deserts. The wind sweeps over it with great power—driving the sand with a force almost sufficient to penetrate the skin.

Friday, June 12th.

Another foggy, rainy day. The wind during the forenoon from the east, in the afternoon calm, in the evening from the west; but the fog still continues. We left Grand Marais River at 8 o'clock and ran before the wind till within about three miles of the Pictured Rocks—a distance of twenty miles. We were afraid that the waves would prevent our landing if we proceeded further, as they were already pretty high and the wind increasing. The *"Chapelle"* is about three miles west of us, and is the commencement of the Pictured Rocks. The process of landing was quite a novelty to a land-lubber like myself. As the bow of the boat touched the sand, the men sprang into the roaring surf, some holding the boat while others first took us on their back to shore, and then took out the loading in the same manner. Then the boat itself had to be hauled up some rods on the beach. After warming ourselves by a good fire and taking some refreshment, we walked almost to *"La Chapelle"*—so called from the resemblance it is said to bear to the front of a church.

The bank, as far as we walked, is very steep and about forty feet high. Toward the end of our walk we found a shore of sandstone rising almost perpendicularly from the water, and worn by the action of the waves into many curious shapes—here forming a snug little bay, there excavating a portion of the rock so as to make a deep cavern. At a distance of about twenty rods from this high rocky shore, is another bluff of nearly the same height. In several places this is also composed of sandstone. And here we saw the most conclusive evidence that this bluff had once been the shore of the lake, at a time when it was full fifty feet above its present level. It shows the same marks of having been beaten by the surf as are exhibited by the rocks against which the waters are now dashing. The base of the rock is worn away very much, and here and there is a deep cavern, in which are the round stones of the beach. There is something peculiar in the appearance of a sandrock worn by water which cannot be mistaken. How long is it since the rolling wave last roared into these coves and licked their smallest recesses with its pliant tongue? Since the second day's work when the waters were divided from the waters.

Saturday, June 13th.

The forenoon has been rainy and foggy. We have had an immense deal of such weather since we started. We breakfasted at La Chapelle this morning. It stands on the sandrock, about 2 miles west of where it first appears, and one mile from where it assumes the character of "Pictured Rocks." La Chapelle is a portion of these rocks; the softer parts of which have been worn away, leaving it in the shape of a costly temple. The front of this "house not made by hands" is supported by two large perpendicular columns, varying in diameter from five to ten feet. They are the workmanship of the elements, and lose nothing when compared with the labors of man. They are handsomely rounded; the strata of the rock give them the appearance of having been built of hewn blocks. The distance between them is thirty two feet. On the south side (the front being west) are three columns of the same description; except that, as the ground rises towards the rear, the back columns are much shorter. The east end is open like the front, while the north side is entirely closed with rock about ten feet in thickness. From the tops of these columns springs the arch which forms a perfect vaulted roof, projecting several feet beyond the columns and forming a rich, heavy cornice. This roof is about six feet thick and not at all leaky. There is some earth on the roof, and out of the centre grows a large straight pine for a spire. But I believe there is no bell growing there as yet. There is, however, in the body of the church a very convenient pulpit. We remained here till two o'clock. The afternoon was delightfully pleasant, and we proceeded leisurely on our voyage. In a few minutes we came to La Portal, or the door. It is but little over a mile from La Chapelle. It is a promontory of rock, projecting into the lake about five hundred feet, from two to four hundred feet in width, and over two hundred in height. It is broader at the top than at its base and overhangs the water all around, but not much. On the north and south sides are two large caverns which meet near the centre & form a complete tunnel. Another and a larger cavern penetrates the rock in front till it intersects the others. At the point of intersection the arch is just high enough to pass a common yawl boat. This last cave is 100 feet high and the same in width, and about 200 feet deep. We rowed our boat into it and sat for some time admiring the perfect regularity of its vast concave, and listening to the echo of our voices. On firing a gun, which I did twice, the reverberations were almost deafening. The Pictured Rocks extend from a point one mile east of LaChapelle to the western part of Grand Island, a distance of about fifteen miles. There are but two places where it is possible to get on shore—La Chapelle & Miner's River. With these exceptions, the coast is solid perpendicular rock; and woe to the voyageur when he is caught there by a rude Northwester. The rock, sometimes overhanging the water and sometimes receding from it, varies in height from fifty to two hundred feet—probably averaging a hundred and fifty. That portion which is stained by the colouring matter that oozes out between the strata, lies between a line a little above the centre and a line about 15 feet above the surface of the water. The colouring is certainly a great curiousity; but to my eye by no means the most interesting feature of the rock. The colours are, however, in many places very bright, and of every hue and shade imaginable, from jet black to spotless white. By drawing a little on the fancy one can see as he glides past them almost anything he chooses. There is a fine landscape; there are a thousand Indians dancing together in mad carousal; yonder is a battle field strewn with the slain, and the blood still fresh upon the grass; and still farther on is a walled city with its battlements and towers. But the architecture of the rocks is far more admirable than the painting. From one end to the other is a continued succession of deep caverns and the most beautiful arches and pillars. Enormous mountains of rock rest on neatly rounded, tapering columns of stratified rock, which seem to have no other formation than the fickle wave! It is not in Niagara to equal them in beauty though it may surpass them in grandeur. Two or three little streams pour over the tops of the rocks, forming beautiful cascades; and in one of the caverns we noticed a quantity of snow which has not yet felt the heat of a summer sun. We encamped quite early at the mouth of Miner's River, and caught brook trout enough to satisfy our hunger. This is a small, quick stream, and famous as a camping ground where the voyageurs in olden times were often weatherbound, and have left their mark on many a tree.

THE CASTLES, PICTURED ROCKS—*from* Report on the Geology of the Lake Superior Land District, *by* *J. W. Foster* *and* *J. D. Whitney.*

Grand Island, Presque Isle and Points West

Sunday, June 14th.

By three o'clock we were up, and soon after under-way. Five hours are all we get for sleeping, and they are by no means all spent in unbroken slumber. It takes one some time to get familiar enough with the cold ground to sleep soundly upon it. Dreams continually haunt the imagination, but they are all of a pleasant character. It seemed at first quite droll, after reveling all night in the sweets of eastern life, to wake up on the wild shores of Lake Superior. It is rather strange that, when a thousand new and interesting scenes engross all my attention while awake, I should no sooner close my eyes than home, old friends and by-gone times are all before me. But a truce to the philosophy of dreams.

We breakfasted on the south-west point of Grand Island. This island is about 8 miles from North to South, and five from east to west. The interior of the island is high and the shores on the South-east show the pictured rock much like those on the main-land. The shores exhibit sandrock on all sides of the island. The channel which separates it from the main-land is from two to five miles wide. We crossed over to the main-land about 10 o'clock and laid by to keep Sunday, but the service being rather dull and the weather very fine, went on in the afternoon to Au Train River and encamped for the night. It is rather a pretty stream, and into the head of a bay about five miles deep. The west bank affords the handsomest camping ground we have yet seen. It spreads off into a large undulating plain, free from underbrush, and planted like a park with large pine trees. Some of these pine groves are perfect beauty. In fact the whole coast of the lake is one extensive grove, in which the whole family of evergreens is beautifully blended. After passing Grand Island the scenery becomes more wild, and move in accordance with my previous notions of the undisturbed works of nature. The rocks exhibit stronger marks of violence and seem to have been deposited in a more irregular manner. Au Train River is about fifteen miles from Miner's River.

Monday, June 15th.

How cold the nights are! One can hardly keep warm with a heavy overcoat and two good blankets. The thermometer stood below 40°; almost down to the freezing point. But when the sun has been up three or four hours he begins to make himself felt; and by noon it is as hot as in southern latitudes.

The country we have seen to-day is comparatively of little interest. The shore has been generally low and in many places sandy. The red sandstone still shows itself, but its character is somewhat changed. It is much harder, and is mixed with felspar, mica and quartz. We encamped on the east side of Chocolate River, having traveled—following the windings of the coast —about 30 miles. This is the largest stream we have passed since leaving White Fish Point, and is the boundary between United States and Indian lands—the country west of this not having been yet ceded by the Indians. Since we landed I have caught a trout, eaten my supper and written my journal; and now I am ready for blanket.

Tuesday, June 16th.

We are now in a region where the geologists begin to work. We have parted company with the sandstone, and got among hills as high and as rocky as those of New England. About two miles from Chocolate River we ascended a hill [possibly Mt. Mesnard], and spent all the forenoon examining it. It is composed of primary rock; not granite, but the next thing to it. At the base of the rock is found talc-slate, horn-blende and several other minerals. The top of the rock is composed almost entirely of white quartz, and is elevated near three hundred feet above the lake. The upper surface of the rock is worn, as if immense weights had been drawn over it. It is almost as hard as flint, and consequently retains perfectly all these little creases, hollows and scratches. The line of these scratches is from N. E. by E. to S. W. by S. It is supposed that vast bodies of earth and transition rock were once swept over these heights and deposited in various places.

In the afternoon we traveled two miles farther and fixed our city at the mouth of "La Rivere des Morts," or dead river—so called because its banks have long been a place of burial for the Indians. Here we had great sport catching trout. We took fifty in little over an hour,—some of them very large, being about 14 inches long and weighing, as near as I could judge, a pound and a half. They are all meat, and I might almost say ready cooked, for our men clean & cook them before they are fairly dead. I have sat down and eaten one of them, well cooked, that fifteen minutes before was swimming free in the river.

Wednesday, June 17th.

We have had another rainy day. The storms here seem to be accompanied with more thunder than in any other portion of the State. The Doctor says it is a thundering country. We have been confined to our tents the greater part of the day; but caught some trout & killed a duck. We have also seen some red deer, but as they were never known to be in these parts before we are not provided with a rifle or ball to shoot them. Heretofore the caribou, or reindeer have been the only kind seen in so high a latitude. Our men completed to-day the net which Dr. Houghton ordered made, to catch whitefish and Mackinaw trout! It is a set-net and is in the water to-night for the first time. If it answers our expectations, we shall laugh and grow fat, and save some pork besides; long to breed a famine. We went up the river this afternoon in our smallest boat and found it very rapid—as swift in many places as the Sault Ste. Mary. When the current was too strong for us, the men would jump into the water and haul us up. They are admirable water dogs.

Thursday, June 18th.

A Delightful Morning—pure air and bright sun; and, what added materially to our enjoyment, we found two noble whitefish and a trout in our net. What a feast did we make of breakfast & dinner. Stayed in camp all the forenoon—busied in reading and writing, and assisting the Doctor with his minerals. In

ENTRANCE TO GRAND ISLAND HARBOR, PICTURED ROCKS—*from Report on the Geology of the Lake Superior Land District by J. W. Foster and J. D. Whitney.*

the afternoon we embarked, after a stay of two days, and proceeded almost to Presque Isle where we went on shore and encamped for the night. Capt. Johnson soon after arrived and encamped at the same place, on his way from Le Ance [L'Anse] to the Sault Ste. Mary's. We were mistaken in calling the river where we were yesterday the Des Morts.[24] This is the true Des Morts; and the other is not laid down on either of our maps. The two rivers are nearly of equal size and not to exceed five miles apart. I wrote three letters to send by Capt. Johnson— one to E. Penny, one to A. Hartshorn[25] & one to S. Ashman. Pens flew lively for a short time, and we soon made up a package of seven letters. Between these two rivers is Granite Point,[26] jutting out into the lake a quarter of a mile, composed of high ledges of a species of granite in which horn-blende takes the place of mica.

Friday, June 19th.

Our encampment has not been changed to-day. In the forenoon the geological corps went onto Presque Isle and remained until 2 o'clock examining the different strata of rock. The examination is not yet completed; but they found, in what is called the lower sandstone, lead, iron and sulphate of copper and brought off many very good specimens. They also found asbestos. These minerals seem to be strangely mixed together. In a piece of the rock three inches square, the iron pyrites seem to be diffused through the mass, while the other minerals appear in small, detached quantities. There is considerable portion of copper in the vein, but not enough to warrant any experiment of mining. The vein containing these minerals occurs at the junction of the red sandstone and trap rocks, about a mile north of the mouth of River Des Morts. The Doctor brought away about 150 pieces of rock. In the afternoon we ascended the river a mile and a half, when we came to a rapid that stopped our boat. The river leapt along over a ledge of granitic rock, or gneiss rock, and falls about twenty feet in a quarter of a mile.

---

[24]On the previous day they had camped at Carp River.

[25]This may have been Alfred Hartshorn, who, according to the 1837 Detroit directory, resided on Fort St. above Shelby St.; his occupation was not given. No other Hartshorn was listed.

[26]Granite Point is now known as Lighthouse Point in the city of Marquette, Mich., where a light was established in 1853.

The water over some portion of the rock was shallow, so that we could walk through it. On these rocks we found quantities of *Carp,* or Suckers, and we immediately soused in and began to catch them with our hands. It was grand sport. The water roared and foamed around us and the inequalities of the rock rendered a foothold rather uncertain. But we cared little for wetting. The suckers would gather in the deepest holes in the rock, and we stationed ourselves around to prevent their escape. In a short time we had caught thirty-five of the largest kind. But they are so much inferior to our whitefish & trout that we cannot think of eating them. The country on the river, as far as we went is worthless, being alternate sandridge & marsh. Farther back among the hills, it looks much better. There is an abundance of sugar maple in the valleys and a farmer could live there very well. We killed two ducks & returned. Then came the packing of minerals, which is no small job, as each piece has to be dried, labeled and wrapped in a piece of paper. The Doctor has already put up 6½ barrels of them.

Saturday, June 20th.

This morning early the whole party went upon Presque Isle. The extreme eastern point of the island bears east-N. E. from the mouth of River Des Morts—distant one mile. The island is high and covers an area of about five hundred acres. It is thickly covered with a small growth of birch, maple, poplar, pine & cedar, and is connected with the main-land by a narrow marshy strip of land, almost destitute of trees. On the east the red sandstone & trap rocks meet; rising abruptly from the water to a height of 40 or 50 feet. The sandstone is curiously curved, and has at some time been shattered into innumerable fragments, and the interstices filled with an injection of quartz quite bare and prominent, resembling the small roots of a tree, thickly interwoven and washed white by the water. The trap has the most forbidding aspect of all rocks. It is almost black, full of irregular fissures and uneven upon its surface. It was undoubtedly thrust up, in a fluid state through the granitic formation, which was broken and upheaved from its original bed. Dykes are thrown up through openings in the granite, filling the space as perfectly as though it had been melted wax. There is abundant

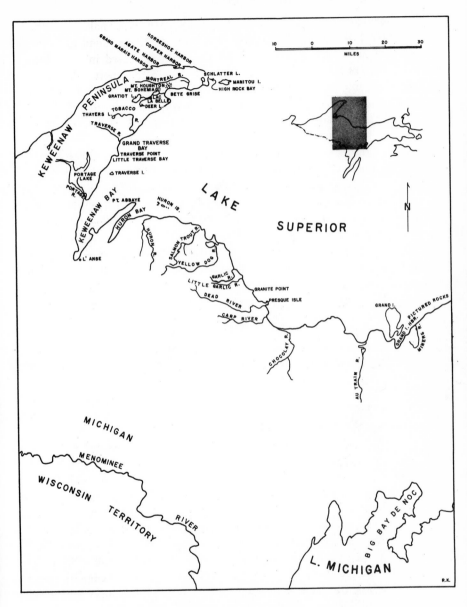

MAP II — *Central Upper Michigan and the
Keweenaw Peninsula, 1840.*

evidence that these masses of rock have once been melted "with fervent heat," aside from the similarity which exists between them and the lava which boils in the craters of volcanoes at the present day.

In the afternoon we embarked, and proceeded to the west side of Granite Point where we encamped at the mouth of a small stream [Harlow's Creek], the name of which we have not yet learned. It empties into the lake about five miles N. W. of the river—Des Morts. Granite Point [Little Presque Isle] is a knob of granite about thirty feet high connected with the land by the red sandstone. It is almost an island as the strip of sandstone is not over four rods in width. On our way we landed and ascended one of the highest knobs of granite we have yet seen.[27] It is very steep and we had some difficulty in getting to the top. But the view we obtained well repaid our labor. Some five or six islands lie scattered in the lake before us, while far in the distance appeared the dim outlines of Grand Island and the Pictured Rocks. In the west rose a succession of granitic knobs, one above another as far as the eye could extend. These peaks are sharp and but scantily covered with scrubs of evergreen. They lie in something like regular ranges, which bear from North by west to south by east. The knob we were on measured four hundred and fifty feet in height.

Sunday, June 21st.

We have had a day of rest—a sabbath in the wilderness. A clear sky, bright sun and brisk north-west wind rendered it pleasant as heart could wish; and yet we were not content without our fire. No one has strayed away from camp, for a walk in the wild woods has ceased to be a novelty. We read the Bible I dare say much more than we would have done had we been in Detroit. Shakespeare was duly honored, as he is every day when we travel. When on the water some one of the party usually reads his plays to the others. But our time was not wholly occupied in reading. Each had a little writing to do, a little overhauling of trunks, a few rips & rents to sew up; and

---

[27]The hill was known to the Indians as Tatosh, meaning "Woman's Breast," and is now called Sugar Loaf (elevation above sea level, 1,077 ft.).

for myself I had a small washing to attend to. Some of my
clothing had long been mourning "in dust and ashes" for the
washtub; and so I tied them together and anchored them on a
rock amidst the dashing waves. They were kept in constant
motion and by the middle of the afternoon were quite clean. I
stretched my fish line from tree to tree and hung my clothes up.
Thus the waves washed and the wind dried them. But who
will do the ironing? Ah! there's the rub. I shall have to put
them between my blankets and lie on them.

Monday, June 22nd.

Doctor Houghton and his assistants spent the morning in
taking some instrumental observations of the sun and moon;
and in examining the rocks in the neighborhood. They are similar to those we passed on Saturday, and curious only in their geological character. Before noon we embarked, keeping along the
coast, with a gentle favorable breeze. We stoppd at Garlic
River, an inconsiderable stream, and took dinner; after which
we continued our course to the mouth of Pine [Salmon Trout]
River, passing St. John's[28] River without stopping, and encamped about sunset. We have advanced to-day about 20 miles.
The coast shows the red sandstone most of the way with an
occasional knob of granite. The trap rock has not been seen
since we left Garlic River. The country as far as we could see
back from the lake is covered with sharp hills [Huron Moun-
tains], which are composed almost entirely of granite. Opposite
our encampment are three or four Indian lodges. The old chief
came over and, after eating some supper and receiving a present
of tobacco, sat and smoked the pipe of peace with us till near
eleven o'clock. He ate very sparingly of what was set before
him for supper—putting most of the hardbread and pork into
a corner of his blanket for his children. So it seems an Indian
is not destitute of parental feeling, notwithstanding the number
of his wives. The rugged and bold outlines of Point Keweenaw
stretching away into the lake, are plainly seen from this place—

---

[28]Penny is referring to the Yellow Dog River, a translation of the earlier French name, Riviére Chien Jaune. "Chien Jaune" apparently
sounded like "Saint John" to English-speaking travellers, and the
stream was often labeled the St. John River on early maps and in early
accounts.

distant about thirty miles. They do not appear more than 10 or 15 miles away, and their appearance is singular enough. One moment you can see them distinctly—the next they are melted into thin air, and presently you begin to see their tops hanging in the air, like the baseless fabric of a vision. I never saw such an instance of the refraction of light.

Tuesday, June 23rd.

There was nothing to invite the attention of a geologist in the neighborhood of Pine River, consequently, after a short excursion, the Doctor returned, having killed a porcupine, which we had served up at supper. The flavor of the meat is not unpleasant; but there was something about it that reminded me so strongly of *very young veal* that I shall say nothing in its favor. We went over to the Indian lodges; and I am more and more convinced that Indians, in their natural state, are not the miserable beings which they become when brought into immediate contact with the whites. The girls were all dressed in red frocks, and the boys, with the exception of a few that had taken off their clothes, were dressed much more decently than the children of poor people in cities. In the forenoon we moved on as far as Huron River, against a stiff head wind. This is a larger stream than most that we have passed; and might be classed with the Twin [Two-Hearted] and Chocolate for size. It is eight miles west of Pine River. Although the day has been perfectly clear, and we are 8 miles nearer, yet we can scarcely see the hills of Point Keweenaw. They seem to be at least fifteen miles farther off than they did last night. Most of our party have been up the river this afternoon, but discovered nothing of consequence, while I remained in camp. The banks of the river on the east side are high and very pleasant—a frate charm[29] for a village. It has been an old Indian burying ground, and I noticed three graves of white people covered over with pine logs over which is erected a cross. One bears date "Augt. 1822," one 1833, and the date of the other is illegible. The Indians pay great respect to their dead & renew the covering to their graves often.

---

[29]This was a slang expression of the era, meaning a "beautiful site."

L'Anse and the Keweenaw Country

Wednesday, June 24th.

Soon after breakfast we set sail, the wind being favorable, for the American Fur Co's post at Le Ance. We made a traverse of six miles, across the mouth of Seepeeweeshee [Huron] Bay to Point Abbaye, which is by the traders pronounced *Obain*. This narrow bay extends fifteen miles into the land running parallel with Keweenaw Bay, and being separated from it by a strip of land from three to five miles wide by twenty in length, on the west side. After doubling Point Abbaye the wind was directly aft, blowing fresh, and we were in much doubt whether to proceed or not. But we kept on and, the wind increasing, we soon had a heavy sea to ride. The waves I think were higher than any I ever saw in Lake Erie, without a much heavier wind. By two o'clock we were at the wharf of the American Fur Co. having sailed near thirty miles. We find the agent of the company, Mr. [Ambrose] Davenport, very sociable and polite to our party. He gives freely all information respecting the surrounding country that he possesses, and relates many anecdotes of his early adventures in this country. There are a great many Indian graves at this place, and some of them highly decorated. Three or four have houses built over them in the form of large tombs. Within these tombs they offer to the dead the first fruits of the season—the first mocock of sugar, first fish taken &c.—and we found in one of them a basket of strawberries. On the outside were hung bells, furs, eagle quills, scalps and many other of their trophies and manufactures. The scalps were taken last season from their ancient enemies the Sioux. The Chippeways have sent out a war party this summer against the Sioux, but nothing has yet been heard from them. Among the scalps was a complete skin of a pe-chau-guin,[30] hung over the grave of a girl of seventeen. On this grave flowers are frequently strewn. About half a mile south of the trading post is a large deposit of Novaculite. Some of it is very fine—almost equal to the Scotch Ayre stone for a razor or knife. The grit of some portions is very sharp, and would make superior stones for the ax or scythe. The Indians cut pipes out of it, though they greatly prefer the red pipe-stone. We parted company with the Doctor yesterday morning. With his light boat he coasted round Huron, or Seepeeweeshe, Bay, thus lengthening his day's journey about thirty miles. He rejoined us, however, contrary to our expectations, this evening before nine o'clock.

Thursday, June 25th.

Mr. Davenport sent us this morning fresh fish, potatoes and milk. The potatoes tasted sweeter than sugar plums to children; and we have quite a bag full for future use. They have oxen, horses & cows, and raise plenty of potatoes every season. I think the climate at the head of this bay must be milder than at Mackinaw. Keweenaw Bay is about 20 miles deep, and about fifteen miles wide at its mouth, gradually becoming narrower as you approach the head where it is between two & three miles wide. The trading post of the American Fur Co. is situated on the east side of the bay, about three miles from the head. The Methodists have established a Mission some two miles farther down the bay. They have selected a very handsome spot, and built ten or twelve small houses, which give it the appearance of a village. The place, however, was deserted when we were there; not a human being, or dog even, was to be seen. The Indians were scattered in different directions for the purpose of fishing, and there is at present no school at the Mission to take charge of the children while the men are absent.

The American Fur Co. pays the Indians four dollars a barrel for putting up fish—the Co. furnishing barrels & salt only. They also pay the Indians a very high price for turs—twelve shillings for Martin skins, each, & four dollars a pound for beaver skins. But they pay them in flour at from ten to twenty dollars the barrel; powder, two dollars per pound, & three shil-

---

[30]Penny was probably speaking of a cow hide or buffalo robe. Rev. Frederic Baraga, in his *Dictionary of the Ochipwe Language*, gives the spelling as *pijikiwegin*.

lings for shot. Blanket and dry goods pay an equally good profit. We spent almost the entire day coasting round the head of the bay and examining the rocks, which are mostly of a clay slate, and broken sandstone. There is no indication of a deposit of any kind of ore. We found a vein of beautiful white quartz and the Doctor obtained a number of large crystals. We also spent considerable time in examining the vein of Novaculite, mentioned yesterday. It is not so fine as I was led to suppose by the account given of it by the inhabitants. It breaks very much in quarrying—and it is difficult to work out a good piece. We brought away a few specimens and our men worked out some very good whet stones. The grit is too coarse for a razor but answers well for common knives.

Friday, June 26th.

Every appearance of the weather this morning was indicative of a storm; but we broke up our camp and, by ½ past 5 were under way for the mouth of Portage River. This is on the opposite side and down the bay—and distant but fifteen miles, yet the wind was so strong ahead that it was eleven o'clock before we arrived and got our breakfast. Immediately after eating we again proceeded on down the coast. We had not been out long when the wind increased, and the waves became so high as almost to stop our head way; but we found it impossible to land. We continued on till nine o'clock in the evening when we got ashore and encamped in a small bay called "Baye du Grese," [actually Little Traverse Bay], about twelve miles N. E. of the mouth of Portage River. The coast for twenty miles back is the most dangerous we have yet passed. It is one continued ledge of red sandstone rock, and swift destruction is the inevitable fate of any barge that may chance to be thrown against it. Our men are pretty well sobered, having tugged hard at the oar for fifteen hours—stopping but once.

Saturday, June 27th.

On examination this morning we found ourselves in a large sandy bay which in no wise answered to the description given us of Baye du Grese. A small stream [Mud Lake Creek] empties itself into the head of the bay, but after following up its course as far as our smallest boat could go, we were not forty rods from shore; the stream runs so nearly parallel with the bay. We embarked about 1 o'clock, and after proceeding three miles entered another sandy bay [Grand Traverse Bay] into which a stream of a larger size usually empties.[31] I say *usually* for the mouth had been entirely closed by the waves yesterday, and we were obliged to haul the boat over the dam. The dam had raised the water in the river between two and three feet, which had set back for several miles and covered the marshes. Large streams are frequently stopped in that way, and sometimes find an outlet far from their former mouths. This river was followed up with no better success than the other; except that we caught an enormous great turtle, of some twenty pounds weight. On the return of the boat we made an opening in the sand bank, and it was a beautiful sight to see the water rush into the lake, carrying in its rapid current millions of sparkling particles of sand, and soon excavating a channel broad and as deep as that of some mighty river. We again embarked and after going some 8 miles, came to Tobacco River, called Cascade on our maps on account of a fall which is visible from its mouth. Here we found two families of Indians engaged in fishing. We made but a short stop and proceeded on to a long deep bay—having high rocky mountains on the north and west—and encamped. This is some 7 miles from Tobacco River, is the true Baye du Grese and seems to form the line of separation between the level & the hilly country. The coast thus far has been quite uniform. The old red sandstone is seen all the way, except where the coast is here and there indented with a small sandy bay. No other rock makes its appearance, and there is not the least sign of a deposit of mineral substance. But we are now in the neighborhood of high rocky mountains, and it will be our business next week to ascertain what hidden mines of wealth are emboweled within them. Now for sleep.

Sunday, June 28th.

Our camp meeting has been as well attended to-day as usual. We have had a fine illustration of the changeable and stormy character of the weather. Last night it rained—in the morning

---

[31] Apparently this was the Traverse River or the outlet of Deer Lake in what is now Houghton County, Mich.

MOUNT HOUGHTON, LAC LA BELLE — *from* Report on the Geology of the Lake Superior Land District *by J. W. Foster and J. D. Whitney.*

the sun shone pleasantly two or three hours—then we had a steady fall of rain till three o'clock, then for three hours the atmosphere was clear & pleasant, & then we had in succession two heavy thunder showers from the west. Between three and four o'clock, I walked out to the eastern cape of the bay where the surf was rolling upon the rocky shore. The opportunity was so good, that I could not resist the temptation of bathing in the surf; so I stript off my clothing and walked into the edge of the water. The first breaker nearly took away my breath and gave me such a shock that I could hardly stand. After receiving the third or fourth I was obliged to go on shore to breathe; but I soon returned to the encounter and took another round. The water is very cold and, after the first shock, produces a great reaction of the blood. The skin all over my body became as red as a ripe cherry. This morning the Doctor called for a looking glass, there being but one small one in the party, and said he wanted I should see how like the Devil I looked. O! horror of horror! Is that Penny! C. W. Penny! "I'll look no more, lest my brain turn." Is it possible that wild beasts shun me? I should think they would claim me for a relative. But perhaps they take me for a more savage species than themselves and betake them to flight for safety. We dined at ½ past five on turtle—boiled, fried and souped—quite a feast. I have made acquaintance with several new dishes since I left Detroit; to wit: speckled trout, sea gull, porcupine, muskrat and river turtle all in their place; but, were it not for the name, I quite as lief would have wild turkeys. I have nothing, however, to complain of, on the score of eating. My appetite gives a relish to everything. Nor do we want for variety. In addition to the game we get and our ample store of provisions, we have a good supply of the finest fish. Night before last we caught three whitefish and one trout; last night two large whitefish. One can never get tired of them in this latitude. The meat is so fine, hard and white, and so sweet, that all other fish seem "flat, stale and unprofitable" when compared with them.

Monday, June 29th.

The air has been clear, with the exception of a very singular driving mist that occasionally appeared like fog and wet us as fast as ordinary rain. It has been cold enough to make us keep a good fire all day. Not a fly has troubled us. In the forenoon the Doctor went around into the head of the bay [Bete Grise], and ascended for a short distance a river which empties into it.[32] On his return we removed our camp to the mouth of the river, which brought us within a mile of the highest range of mountains. This bay is some two and a half miles deep, and lessens the width of the [Keweenaw] Point about that much. It seems to be the end of a wide strip of low land which lies between the range of hills and coast from the mouth of Portage River to this place. Mr. F. Hubbard and myself measured the height of the two highest points of the mountain in our neighborhood and found one 872, & the other 878 feet.[33] The Doctor and his assistant dispersed in different directions to get the outline of the geology of the rocks. Judging from their reports we have very little prospect of finding copper anywhere near our present position. Certain it is we have not yet seen copper enough to turn green.

Tuesday, June 30th.

This morning we ascended the river, keeping nearly parallel with the range of hills. About two miles above the mouth we entered a lake [Lac La Belle], two miles in length by ¾ of a mile in breadth—a beautiful sheet of water—clear and deep. On the N.W. side rose the highest mountain we have yet seen (878) which we ascended; and from the top obtained a full view of the Point.[34] The south-eastern shore was visible in its entire length, and we could see ten or fifteen miles of the coast on the other side. Point Keweenaw is divided by a ridge of mountains which passes along about four miles back of the eastern shore. Near the western & northern side runs a parallel ridge of nearly equal height. Between them is a valley some four or five miles wide, thickly covered with maple, birch, oak and evergreens. The hills are also very thickly wooded. About ½ a

---

[32]The stream was the outlet of Lac La Belle, now known as the Mendota Ship Canal.

[33]Penny may have been referrng to Mt. Houghton (elevation 877 ft.; 1,477 ft. above sea level).

[34]This possibly was Mt. Bohemia (elevation 864 ft.; 1,467 ft. above sea level).

mile south of the lake already mentioned lies one of much less size [Deer Lake, Keweenaw County], and about six miles southwest we could see one [Gratiot Lake] of three or four miles extent, lying near the hills. The last mentioned is probably the source of Tobacco River.[35] We were unable to follow the river beyond the first lake on account of flood wood.

Wednesday, July 1st.

We proceeded this forenoon leisurely along the coast, which differs from any we have yet passed, and encamped at the mouth of Cascade [Little Montreal] River—distant from Bay du Gres seven miles. Midway are some rocky mountains from 400 to 500 feet high—rising almost perpendicularly from thé shore. The rocks, of which they are composed, and which form the whole extent of coast we have passed to-day, are a fused conglomerate of sandstone—called in geological language Trap Tuff. From the slight examination we were able to give it to-day, the Doctor is unable to say much of the character of its minerals. It is to undergo a close scrutiny to-morrow. I noticed as we passed that a large portion of the forest trees is poplar, with maple, birch and oak—the evergreens having almost disappeared. The coast lies in nearly an east and west direction. The Cascade is quite a smart stream; and rushes over a bed of rocks into the lake. The fall is some 12 to 15 feet. Sailing along the shore this morning we rescued a whitefish from the jaws of an otter and appropriated it to our own. It was a very fine one, length 29 inches, circumference 17, weight 12 pounds. He was almost round, and nearly of equal size from head to tail. Last night we caught two in our net, and shot two ducks and a muskrat. Our market is tolerably well supplied with fish.

Thursday, July 2nd.

By examining the rocks on the coast this morning we found what is called copper black, green oxyd of copper & Malachite. The first vein occurs about three-fourths of a mile west of the mouth of Little Montreal, or Cascade, River. There are three or four veins, the farthest west of which lies about a mile & a quarter from the river. The Doctor considers them perfectly

---

[35]Thayer Lake, not Gratiot Lake, is a source of the Tobacco River.

valueless for mining purposes; and of no further consequence other than they show the probable extent of some veins on the other side of the Point. He brought away quite a number of specimens of the ore and the rock in which it is contained, and is unwilling to pronounce decidedly its character till he has analyzed it. A few rods west of these veins rises an almost perpendicular ledge of rock to a height of 4 to 500 feet. It is composed of Tropean Silicious Slate, hard and compact and perfectly destitute of minerals. In the afternoon we started, with the intention of going as far as Copperas Harbor, but stopped at a place called by the French, Grand Marais, and encamped.[36] It is a singular, but perfectly secure harbor for batteaux. A detached line of rock 15 feet high, lies in front; between which, and a similar ledge which forms the shore, we pass along for a quarter of a mile in a channel of twenty-five feet width, and then turn—through a small aperture of the rock —into a little bay, or lake, that cannot be seen from the lake. It is formed something in this manner.

This rock is an altered conglomerate, and that is the character of a great portion of the rock we have passed to-day. On the extreme point of the peninsula, the rock was originally the same, but has been completely melted, and might be termed sandstone trap. The land around the point is raised about 12 feet and perfectly level. It is composed chiefly of small angular pebbles, and was once covered with a fine growth of pine timber which appears to have been destroyed by a drought. It is now overspread with young maple, poplar, &c. Its appearance was very handsome, and one could scarcely desire a more pleasant summer retreat. We saw three deer walking leisurely upon the beach, and wounded a buck very severely, but he made his escape.

About three miles (or perhaps I should say from *one* to *three* as I don't know the spot) after leaving Montreal River, the Doc-

---

[36]Grand Marais (Little Grand Marais Harbor), in what is now Keweenaw County, Mich., is approximately seven miles *west* of Copper Harbor. Penny may have mistaken a small, similarly-shaped bay, just east of Horseshoe Harbor, for Grand Marais. This small bay is about 3.5 miles *east* of Copper Harbor, and would fit his description of Grand Marais quite well. He may have been describing High Rock Bay, but this is unlikely, as it is farther east and not protected by rock formations.

tor struck upon a vein of copper ore which frớm a slight examination he thinks may be valuable. Owing to some misunder-
standing between him and ourselves, our boat did not stop,
which I regret the more as it prevented the Doctor from staying
as long as he wished in order to satisfy himself of the extent of
the deposit. He will give it a thorough investigation on his
return; but then I shall not be with him. We are now four
miles from Copperas Harbor, and one day from the fourth of
July; but I wish they were both farther off, for I have a large
boil on my right cheek, and another coming behind my left ear,
which almost makes me crazy. It makes my head & teeth ache;
and I suppose I might as well sit up and write till morning as
undertake to sleep. These boils may be owing to the ague &
fever, or, what is more likely, to my present manner of living.
My food has been principally meat and very rich fish—my appetite keen, and my belly fat. Distance traveled to-day, twelve
miles.

Friday, July 3rd.

We were not long in ascertaining that no minerals were to
be found near this point; and proceeded early in the day to
Copperas Harbor, distant four miles. This is probably the only
place on Lake Superior that will ever be of value for its minerals. I have been quite sick to-day with my boils; confined
most of the time to my tent. I accompanied the party, however, to the vein, and remained long enough to satisfy myself,
as far as one can judge of appearances, that copper in this vein
is worth something. The Doctor & his assistants remained
there all day to clear away the rubbish and blow out some of the
ore. He wishes to open the vein a little below the surface of
the water but his blasting tubes were so faulty that after three
or four unsuccessful attempts he was obliged to return to camp
without having accomplished anything. This vein of copper is
on the eastern cape, and near the entrance, of Copperas Harbor.
The rock in which it occurs is conglomerate of sandstone, altered by heat. The vein at the water's edge is about twelve
feet wide and rises to a height of four or five feet. It can be
traced, by its colour, several rods into the lake, when the water
suddenly deepens, and we lose sight of it. The vein takes a

south-eastern direction and appears on the other side of the cape. It appears above the ground, at the first mentioned point only two or three rods, and is then covered with the forest; but from the shape of the ground I should think it runs near the surface. It contains pure Malachite, green oxyd, and copper black. The vein is composed of calioruous spar, and these kinds of ore are disseminated through it. Some of the specimens are very rich, while others contain but little metal. Our favorable symptom is, that no native copper has been found in or near the vein. Before the Doctor gets through, I shall probably be able to give some better opinion as to the extent of the deposit. Should there be found sufficient inducement to warrant an ex- periment in mining, there could not be a better place on the lake. The country is fine. The harbor large, always accessible and perfectly secure. The Doctor lanced one of my boils this evening and I feel much easier. I am not disposed to complain, but if it had suited all round just as well, it would have suited me much better to have the boils some other time.

Copper Harbor, Saturday, July 4th.

Our mining operations were renewed & continued till 4 o'clock this afternoon. Two blasts were put in near each other, which together threw out about a ton of ore—some of it quite rich. But I shall refrain from any further description of it until the examination is completed. We intend to follow the direction of the vein over the bay and hills and see if any trace of it can be found in the valley that runs up the centre of the peninsula.

The day has been very fine, and celebrated in a manner suitable to the circumstances in which we were placed. Our largest tent was elegantly fitted up for the occasion, shaded and decorated with boughs of evergreen. At five o'clock the pro- cession was formed near the left of the encampment, and marched, headed by the music, the Marshall of the day & stand- ard bearer, through the principal avenues of our beautiful city to the large commodious edifice near the centre of Main St. Here the following exercises took place. Music by the band— "Hail Columbia." Reading, Declaration of Independence by D. Houghton, M.D., P.C., S.G. &c. &c. Oration by B. Hub- bard Esqr., B & A.S.G. Song by F. Hubbard Esqr., Astronomer,

H.S. &c. Benediction by C. C. Douglass, A.S.G. & C.S. We then marched to our large banqueting hall, where a dinner had been prepared in the most sumptuous manner by J. Labille Esqr., chief butler. On the table many kinds of wild fowl, among which were two cedar partridges, (a rare kind of game),[37] several varieties of wild duck & a dozen wild pigeons. Three of the choicest kinds of fish and a few jars of pickled oysters, were among the dainties of the table. After the removal of the cloth —the usual number of regular toasts were drunk in the best of wine, and a much greater number of patriotic volunteers which were received with tremendous cheering. I have not room to give the many excellent sentiments that were drunk, though it is to be hoped that they will be collected and published for the benefit of such of our fellow citizens as were unable to attend. Not an accident occurred to mar the festivities of the day, and though some among us were mellowed with the generous wine there were no exhibitions of drunkeness, or fighting to disgust the senses, or pain to the moral feelings of the most sedate of human kind. Should the annual return of that day bring equal enjoyment I shall never have reason to complain.

Copper Harbor, Sunday, July 5th.

Sunday is always a welcome day; whether in the crowded city, or the wild woods, engaged in the cares & toils of business, or oppressed with the intolerable burthen of idleness, Sunday always brings relief. In such a place as this, how sweetly the thoughts steal away to distant friends—to the favorite few—the *one* bosom friend, when Sunday has stopped the pulse of worldly business! I have been to-day just in that dreamy, ruminating, meditative mood, which may be called the fool's heaven, or the wise man's holyday. To realize this state, one must lay upon an easy couch, between sleeping & waking not caring at which condition he arrives; and then, without the exertion of thinking, he must follow his thoughts whithersoever they lead. The moment he attempts to bridle them the spell is broken. The day has been clear and pleasant. Our men covered the tents with bushes which kept them at the right temperature. One

---

[37]The partridge was probably a spruce grouse, also known as a "fool hen."

of them took my gun and, without going far, killed sixteen pigeons. They are very plentiful and quite tame & fat. My boils have got over their troubles, and I shall henceforth be more careful of my diet. The truth is my body is full of strange humours, that must have vent.

Copper Harbor, Monday, July 6th.

We removed our camp over to the west cape this morning, for the purpose of escaping the torment of flies & mosquitoes and to keep a lookout for vessels. Before noon we saw a schooner bound East, but she either did not see, or disregarded our signals. The forenoon I spent in assisting F. Hubbard to triangulate the harbor, of which we intend to-morrow to have an accurate survey. About 11 o'clock I joined Houghton and his party, who were putting in blasts at the copper mine, and remained with them till 5 o'clock when we adjourned to dinner. Some fine specimens were thrown out; and three ½ barrels filled with them. The only question to be settled about this vein, (which occurs in a fault of the rock some 10 or 12 feet wide), is its extent. The one is of a very excellent quality and is in a most convenient situation for working. After the Doctor has examined the nature of the gang sufficiently & collected what specimens he wants, he intends to search all the rocks on the coast, in the interior and on the mountains, as their structure will in some measure indicate the extent of copper deposit at this place. To-morrow I will have a chart of the harbor, Gull Island and all.

Copper Harbor, Tuesday, July 7th.

Doctor Houghton's examinations at this place were brought to a close to-day, but there is little more to be said relative to the copper ore. Two more blasts were put in, near the water, on the highest point where the ore appears, and a quantity of the best ore thrown out. It is the Doctor's opinion that the vein can be worked to advantage. He thinks it one of the finest places in the world for the manufacture of chemicals—such as Blue Vitriol, Acetate of copper &c., and, that more money could be made out of it that way than by making pure copper. While there, we threw out perhaps five ton of the rock, one-fifth of which was good ore, worth 50 per cent. About one-half of the other four tons contained more or less copper. There were small bits of native copper found in the conglomerate rock in which the vein occurs. The Doctor says there is more of the ore & that the quality is better than he expected to find. Still he thinks the veins, discovered a few miles east of Little Montreal, or Cascade, River will prove most valuable. He says there are three ore veins near each other, and as he becomes better acquainted with the geology of the Point, his confidence in the copper deposits increases. There is a beautiful lake [Lake Fanny Hooe], lying about 300 yards back of Copper Harbor. It is over a mile in length and full ¼ of a mile wide. Its outlet is over a rocky bed and too rapid and shallow to be ascended by boats. But we took our small boat over by land this afternoon, and coasted round the lake, without discovering anything of importance, or interest save an eagle's nest of mammouth dimension—6 feet depth, 3 in breadth. I had the pleasure of shooting thirteen pigeons while walking near the shore. We finished to-day our survey of the harbor; and I think I will attempt to give a chart of it on the next page. Near the western cape is a bare ledge of rocks, where the gulls raise their young, for which reason we call it "Gull Island" [probably Porter's Island]. They keep a constant screaming all night. They have become quite tame, & we catch their young ones every day as they swim about the harbor, but we never harm them. It is now ½ past 10 o'clock & by ½ past three in the morning we expect to be on our way west.

Wednesday, July 8th.

We left Copper Harbor early and renewed our voyage west. The altered conglomerate, interspersed with veins of spar, continued about six miles. The shore that distance is one entire mass of rock, separated portions of which lie off from ten to twenty rods in the water, sometimes so numerous as to form very fine little harbors. There is some little copper ore scattered through the rock, but of no value. Where the rock changes to trap (about six miles from Copper Harbor) there is a bay [Agate Harbor] of over a mile in depth. A long island runs up through the centre which, with four or five small ones near the entrance, gives it very beautiful appearance. The rock west of this is trap for six or eight miles, where we come to a sandy and gravelly beach. The trap which we passed contains agate, but we did not stop to pick out any of them. We have seen four red deer on the beach—they seem to be numerous. We have run to-day near thirty miles, passed Eagle River & a small nameless creek,[38] & are now encamped about 10 miles from Portage River on the round gravel, where mosquitoes are thicker than ever.

Thursday, July 9th.

We embarked early and proceeded to the [Keweenaw] Portage to breakfast. After breakfast we had made but two miles, when a brisk head wind compelled us to lay by four hours; but we made up the loss by rowing till 10 o'clock at night, when we arrived at Misery River & encamped, having made during the day thirty-two miles. About two miles west of the Portage we struck red sandstone, which rises like a wall along the shore for fifteen miles; but there are occasional breaks in it where a boat might be hauled up with safety. This used to be called Carver's River,[39] that celebrated traveler having spent a winter near its mouth. Some years after, however, a party of Frenchmen who came here to spend the winter and trade with the Indians, suffered so severely for want of provisions that they gave its present name to the river. The Indians having left the country, & the Frenchmen being unable to get back, more than half of them perished with hunger. Seven or eight miles back we passed Graveyard River, a small stream where Mr. Graverod,[40] uncle to Mr. G. of Mackinaw, was killed by the Indians 60 or 70 years ago. We saw foot prints of Indians on the sand beach to-day which appeared quite fresh, but no Indians could be seen or heard. Pleasant, comfortable summer weather.

---

[38]Apparently the stream was either the Gratiot River or Hill Creek.

[39]Jonathan Carver (1710-1780) was a native of Connecticut and a noted traveller. He was made a captain in the British Colonial Army in America in 1760. In 1766 he was commissioned by Robert Rogers, Governor of Michilimackinac, to map the major river areas of what are now Wisconsin and Minnesota, preparing for the establishment of a passage to the Northwest. He returned by way of Lake Superior in August of 1767. He wrote of his experiences in an extremely popular book, *Travels Through the Interior Parts of North America in the Years 1766, 1767 and 1768*, which was published in London in 1778. A highly readable account, it went through four translations and 30 editions.

[40]The "Graveyard" River is a corruption of the name Graveraet. It was named for Gerritt Graveraet, a former Detroit merchant who was "broken" by Abraham Cuyler for nonpayment of a debt about 1783. "Mr. G. of Mackinaw" was Henry G. Graveraet, Sr., an interpreter, and son of Gerritt.

At Ontonagon—The Journey to La Pointe

Friday, July 10th.

The lake was perfectly smooth this morning & we were early on our way to the Ontonagon. It was a dead calm, and we felt the heat of the sun more than on any previous day. We reached the mouth of the river at three o'clock having traveled thirty miles. On the west bank is an Indian village of five or six lodges, & on the east an old deserted log house—once occupied as a dwelling and store house. The east bank if cleared up would be very handsome. We rested about an hour & took dinner. As we were rising from our dinner table, seven Indians appeared, headed by a tall powerful fellow, naked and painted in a most hideous manner. We made them some presents of tobacco and hardbread, and proceeded on our way up the river. We had ascended but two miles when we saw two canoes filled with Indians coming rapidly toward us. We stopped and they came alongside and demanded a talk. They said the Old Chief, Buffalo, who had gone to the Ste. Mary's, left orders that no white people must go up the river during his absence, & that we must return to the mouth of the river and await the arrival of the Old Chief. This of course we refused. A long talk ensued during which the Indians became considerably excited and, pointing to a turn in the river said they would not permit us to pass that point. We told them we should pass it, & pass up the river notwithstanding their threats. Finding us determined in our course, they moderated their demands and proposed that, if we would give them a barrel of flour, some hardbread and a keg of pork, they would permit us to proceed. We answered that the manner in which they spoke to us was offensive that we did not come here to buy the privilege of seeing the country, that we would give them nothing by compulsion and that we could be

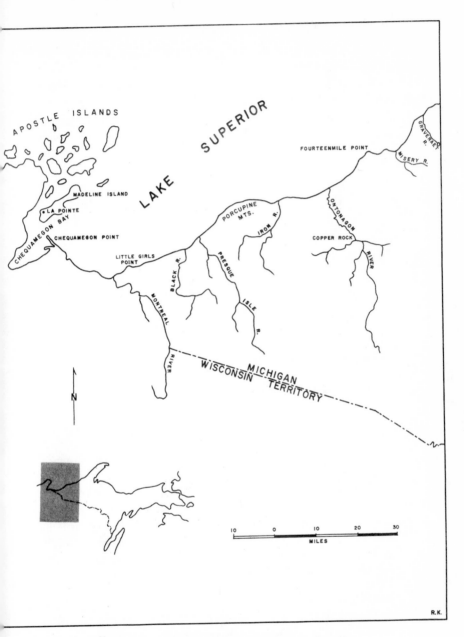

MAP III — *Western Upper Michigan and the*
Apostle Islands area, 1840.

hindered no longer. We then pushed off their canoes & proceeded on. They replied, in a threatening manner, that they would see us when we came back. We encamped on a sandbar about six miles up the river. We have put our guns and pistols in good order and shall keep watch all night. Let an Indian show his head and it will soon be scalpless. But the probability is they have no idea of disturbing us. They thought it would be a fine joke to frighten us out of a little hardbread and pork. Were the Old Chief among them, they would not choose thus to insult us. Three or four of them are as vicious looking a set of devils as live this side of tophet. The young chief (Buff's son) was with them.

Saturday, July 11th.

We found the river this morning so rapid that, after rowing four hours, without making scarce as many miles, we were obliged to fix our encampment and leave the large boat, and all our baggage. We took the small boat, with just pork & bread enough to keep us alive, and went on, but were obliged frequently to get out and walk, while our men hauled the boats over rapids. We arrived at the forks about two o'clock. Here we were obliged to leave the boat and proceed on foot. We started at three o'clock, and after a hard walk over a broken, rugged, hard country, reached the celebrated copper rock at seven in the evening. We lay down on the ground, without tent or blanket and were sung to sleep by mosquitoes. The distance from the forks is computed at six miles, but I think, making all due allowances for the badness of walking and the windings of our way, it must be more. At all events, whoever visits the rock pays well for his curiosity. Nature has seen fit to deposit it in a wild, romantic and perfectly secure place. It can only be taken away when sawed into small pieces, and will probably in time be carried off in the pockets of visitors.

Sunday, July 12th.

By three o'clock this morning all hands were at the rock, eager to obtain a piece of this far famed mineral wonder; but the corners have been so often trimmed before that it required an immense deal of labor to get off even a small bit. It was particularly difficult in my case as the rock hammers and chisels belonged to the Doctor, who was anxious to obtain three or four large pieces for the University and other institutions. He kept the men at work upon the rock till noon, and probably got off twenty-five or thirty pounds. We then started for our boat, steering N.E. by N. over the hills; but this brought us out some two miles below the forks after a walk of three hours. We waited till the men went up and got the boat, when we embarked, and reached our encampment at sunset, tired, wet and hungry. After taking a thumping horn of brandy, eating a huge supper and drying ourselves awhile by the fire we felt quite willing to retire to blanket. Although well satisfied with our trip, we are particularly gratified to know that we shall not have to perform it again.

9 o'clock, Monday, July 13th.

We ran down to the mouth of the river early this morning. The Indians have all decamped; and there is so much wind on the lake that we are unable to put out. So while we are laying by I will try and give a more general description of the country.

For five miles the river is 500 feet broad, with a gentle current. Thence to the forks (20 miles) it is difficult to navigate. We counted twenty-one falls, or rapids, which vary from two to 10 feet. My opinion is that the river descends 100 feet, in its course from the forks to the lake. On each side of the stream are some of the handsomest bottom lands I ever saw, mostly free from underbrush & covered with a magnificent forest of maple, elm, bass wood & oak with scarce a tree of the evergreens. The finest rush beds extend for miles on either side. Above the forks the river foams over a rocky bed and is not navigable by the smallest canoes. The water in some places falls six or eight feet almost perpendicularly. The copper rock lies in the edge of the water on a bed of round stone, on the west side of the west branch of the river distant from the lake about thirty-two miles.

It must be covered with the water more than two-thirds of the year. From the fork it bears, as near as I could judge, S. W. by West. It is within a few feet of the bank, which rises abruptly forty or fifty feet and is covered with trees. The river, a mile or so below, is full of rocks, and turbulent. At one point it rushes through a narrow chasm of the rock which rises over it nearly 100 feet perpendicularly, affording a grand view. All the sandrock, in place, must be passed before reaching the copper. Standing on the mass of copper I could see, a little down the stream and on the opposite side, a bare clay bank about 25 feet high which is the only thing by which I could in any way mark the spot.

Night. We were weather-bound until ½ past 5 o'clock when we got under way and ran ten miles along a sandy beach and encamped at 9 o'clock. We have had pretty much of a Sunday, and have done a large business at washing, mending, ironing and baking. In the afternoon we took a swim in the mouth of the river & found the water warmer than I have ever known it in the Detroit River. We saw no curiosities, unless the graves may be termed so. They are first enclosed in a small house made of boards planed perfectly smooth; over which is a covering of the best birch bark. They are then enclosed within a good sized yard; the pickets are of cedar, set close together and about ten feet high. In one of the yards there are four graves all constructed in the same manner. They were supposed to be the graves of Frenchmen, or half-breeds, each having a cross at the head; but over the newest, we found a bag of corn, some bread, a bouquet of rose flowers and several articles of food, to us unknown, which seemed to indicate that it was the grave of an Indian.

Tuesday, July 14th.

This morning we started at 2 o'clock; but not before daylight. We reached Iron River, a distance of five miles about sunrise. This stream is over a bed of rocks and so full of falls that the smallest canoes can not ascend it more than fifty rods. At the mouth, on the west bank we found Mr. John Bell, a Scotchman who has resided there 10 months. He has built a first rate house, shop and storehouse—all of straight hewn logs; and has a good garden. His business is getting out hoops, which he sells to the American Fur Company on contract; but I did not learn the contract price. He has full blood, little wife; and a boy about two years old—clean and well dressed. In fact her

MASS OF NATIVE COPPER ON THE ONTONAGON RIVER—*from* Narrative Journal of Travels *by* Henry R. Schoolcraft. *Engraved after a sketch by* Mr. Schoolcraft.

house was remarkably clean & neat, and I am told that the squaws, generally, when well treated make excellent housekeepers—"further this deponent sayeth not." Mr. Bell informed us that the Indians from the Ontonagon passed up on Sunday on their way to LaPoint—much chagrined at the ill success which attended their efforts to prevent our passage up the river. Mr. Bell says they had held a number of councils and smokes over the matter, and had been in waiting for us a month—determined to make us pay a contribution. They went there on purpose; and when we passed L'Anse a canoe was dispatched across the portage to let them know we were coming. They tried the same game on Mr. Bell early in the spring—threatening to burn his shop and hoops unless he gave them two barrels of flour, three of corn and one of pork. After spending an hour or two here we went three miles farther and stopped for breakfast. Before we had finished, a head wind sprang up which detained us until 1 o'clock, when we again embarked and ran to Presque Isle River twenty-two miles and encamped. Gentle winds have prevailed from the west & southwest for nearly three weeks. We are probably in the middle of a Lake Superior summer— which seldom lasts beyond the first week of August.

Wednesday, July 15th.

Last night we caught two trout, and had the good fortune to kill a pair of ducks before starting this morning. This is the first fresh cut we have had for a week; and our breakfast and dinner were devoured with the appetites of true voyageurs. We took breakfast at Carp River—six miles from our last night's encampment. The mouth of Carp River is deep & one of the best boat harbors on the coast. There are three or four falls about thirty rods from its mouth, in which is a descent of about twenty-five feet. The rock, above & below the falls, is black slate and worn by the boiling water into many fanciful shapes. On the east bank is an old Indian field & the remains of many lodges &c. On the frame of one lodge were twenty-four beaver skulls tied up very securely, as though of great value. We had scarcely finished our breakfast when clouds of a dark & threatening aspect appeared in different parts of the horizon, and peal after peal of thunder seemed to roll over the lake in all directions. We thought it advisable to remain on shore until the weather should appear more favorable. At noon we started, and had gone but five miles when we were thoroughly drenched by one of those showers which sometimes come too suddenly to be avoided. We were just entering Black river when the rain overtook us. We tarried, however, but a short time, and after rowing till 8 o'clock encamped on the beach at a place called by the voyageurs Point DeFile—in English, Little Girls Point. Whence this name I know not. There is certainly very little resemblance between it and any *point* I have yet seen about a little girl. It is distant from our last night's encampment twenty-seven miles.

Thursday, July 16th.

There was every appearance of rain this morning, but we struck tents at an early hour, and came to the mouth of the Montreal River in time for an early breakfast. The distance is estimated at six miles. Here we have spent the day, which since 9 o'clock has been clear and pleasant. This river is the boundary between Michigan and Wisconsin. It is not over 30 feet in width, and enters the lake through a bed of sandstone which rises on both sides to a height of about 100 feet. Some 40 rods from its mouth it is precipitated over a ledge of rock, and falls from 50 to 60 feet nearly perpendicularly. The river above is full of falls. so much so that the traders in ascending it make a portage of sixty-one miles, or 122 pauses. This brings them to the Wisconsin River, which communicates by another short portage with Lake Du Flambeau. We followed the trail three miles back, which brought us to the top of the high lands elevated 600 feet above the lake. From this point we obtained a grand view of the surrounding miles to the north-west. In the course of the day Mr. Corbin[41] arrived, with six men, three squaws and five children. He made the portage in less than five days, bringing quite a quantity of baggage and about 20 packs of furs. He has two horses with him, in very good flesh, but his Indians carried the heavier burden. We are now at the extremity of Michigan. She terminates with a *fall* which is now roaring in my ears. The coast, however, for the last 30 miles

---

[41]Alexis Corbin was a prominent fur trader.

has been quite uniform. Sandstone, in an almost vertical position, rises from five to 25 feet above the water. On the sandstone rests a stratum of red clay averaging about 25 feet in thickness; and this is covered with a dense forest in which birch greatly predominates. After rambling over the hills and perpetrating a sketch of the falls, I took a long swim in old Superior. The Doctor started for LaPoint at 2 o'clock.

LaPoint—Friday, July 17th.

At two o'clock this morning we left Montreal River and proceeded direct to this place, where we arrived at 12 noon. Capt. Stanard, of the *John Jacob Astor,* arrived last night five days from the Sault Ste. Mary, bringing us three or four letters each & lots of down east newspapers. This is the first intelligence we have received from the Sault since we left there. I had three letters; and never were communications more gratefully received. We expect to remain here till Monday, and have been too busy to look around much as yet. At the first impression I am highly pleased with the location and appearance of the village. It has a most excellent harbor, is on elevated dry ground, and looks clean and wholesome. The American Fur Co. have expended a good deal of labor and money here. They have two large red buildings occupied as a store and storehouse, a good wharf and a fish house two hundred & fifty feet long, besides four or five dwelling houses clap boarded and painted white. The old voyageurs have begun to build considerably and there are about 40 Indian lodges which all together give it the appearance of quite a town. To-morrow I intend to look about and enter in my journal a more ample description. The Indians came about us in large numbers soon after we landed, examining the specimens of different kinds of rock, and laughed heartily to think we should attach value to an article so plenty and valueless. My great, black beard which almost concealed my face, was an object of especial wonder, and procured me the name of *Muck-wa* (Bear) before I had been on shore an hour. Many of them had never seen anything like it before. The Indians uttered a *"ty-yah!"* while the squaws laughed outright, and almost giggled me out of countenance.

Saturday, July 18th.

The rain descended in torrents this morning until the middle of the forenoon. This gave us an opportunity to *shave,* and dress ourselves up in our very best, without the annoyance of visitors. Having performed this very necessary operation, and the weather having become clear, we called upon Doctor Borup, agent of the company; Mr. Okes, agent of the Fond du Lac department; Mr. Bushnell, Indian agent; Mr. Mendonhall, agent of the Northern Lake Company and Mr. Hall, Missionary, all of whom appeared very glad to see us, and invited us to make our home in their houses during our stay & use their offices for writing &c., &c.[42] We accepted an invitation to supper from Doctor Borup, and remained faithful to our engagement. At 6 o'clock we sat down to a table beautifully spread, and graced with the presence of our amiable hostess, Mrs. Okes, two young ladies, daughters of Mr. Okes by a former wife, and Miss McLeod, an accomplished young Scotch lady, who resides with the family as governess. What a luxury it was to drink the best of coffee after an abstinence of two months! How much more delightful to sit down with a circle of intelligent females; and to find ourselves surrounded in a moment with all the luxuries & refinements of civilization. In the evening the young ladies delighted us with some charming music on the piano to which the Doctor added the sweet tones of his violin—a most excellent accompaniment. I have rarely passed a more pleasant evening, or seen a more interesting family.

In the course of the day I made the acquaintance of Mr. Hall, a young graduate of Yale College, who has been traveling alone up the Mississippi as far as St. Peters & the falls of St. Anthony, thence up the St. Croix and down the Bois Brule to Lake Superior. He rambled about with me among the Indian lodges and proved a very companionable fellow. The Indians

---

[42]Penny arrived at La Pointe during the final years of the fur trade, and there he met men who had been with the American Fur Co. many years. The company enjoyed its last prosperous period from 1834 to 1842, when it began to fail. Dr. Charles W. W. Borup was a Danish doctor educated in Copenhagen; he came to America and, as a young man, lived among the Chippewas in the Rainy Lake and Lake Superior country. He later became one of the first bankers in St. Paul, Minn. Charles H. Oakes , who replaced William Atkin as agent at Fond du Lac in 1838, was a member of a family long associated with Lake Superior trade. The Rev. Sherman Hall was a Presbyterian missionary.

all knew me and called me my name, that is *Muck-wa*. They pressed us to enter their lodges and sit down and smoke and talk. In Mr. Bushnell's office I found a rare collection of Indian curiosities. They bestow greater labor on their pipes— some of them being carved into the shape of beasts & birds, with the human face worked into a most comical expression. He challenged me to play chess and I had the honor of beating him a half dozen—easy.

Sunday, July 19th.

This has been a beautiful day. I have been into almost every Indian lodge on the island. The younger portion of both sexes are dressed up in some kind of Sunday finery or other. The girls with bead pantalets, porcupine moccasins, new blue broadcloth shawls, plaited hair and clean faces looked almost good enough to kiss. Most of the women attend church, while a majority of the men visit, smoke and play at some game of chance. They have a tradition, which came down from their forefathers, that the world was once drowned, and the whole human race destroyed with the exception of one man who was a sort of demi-god. He built a great raft on the top of the highest mountain after the water had covered every other spot of earth. The various kinds of animals were saved by swimming to this raft. He saved himself by climbing the highest tree. The waters rose to his feet, then to his knees, his middle and so up, till he could barely keep his nose out of the water. He remained in this situation several days, when an otter swam to him from the raft and dived to the bottom and brought up a small quantity of earth. He kept the otter at work till they had formed a small island, which continued to increase till it, at last, became a continent. The water never subsided but a new earth was formed on its surface. The man, being a Manitou, was capable of producing children of both sexes and thus began a new race of human beings.

There are about 40 lodges, and the Indian population numbers about 300. There are about 46 dwellings, most of which are occupied by old voyageurs, half-breeds &c. The American, French & mixed population numbers near 300. But all the different races are so mingled that a classification would be impossible. From the purest white to the most swarthy complexion there are innumerable shades—"Shade softening into shade and also forming an harmonious whole."

There are four, or five well cultivated farms near the village which produce abundantly. Doctor Borup sent us five bushels of the finest potatoes I ever saw at this season of the year. He says they have more than they know what to do with. They keep a number of cows and have abundance of butter and milk; to the latter article we did ample justice. The ladies (bless their good hearts) insisted on our taking a two gallon jug full, which, by boiling, they said would keep till we arrived at the Sault. We spent the evening with them, but, instead of making a straight walk from their presence to our tents, we proceeded to a large Indian lodge, where the beauty and the chivalry of the forest were assembled in grand dance. The lodge was jammed full but we wiggled our way almost to the centre. Here six girls were dancing to the music of the drum and their own sweet voices. Their feet were kept firmly together, their shoulders covered with blankets and pressed against each other and their only motion that of springing three inches from the ground. The lodge was illuminated with burning tapers of birch bark. The light is brilliant but the tapers are consumed rapidly. Mr. Hubbard and myself got up and began dancing with the girls, but the instant they perceived us they fell as though they had been shot. The Indians set up a great shout and said the girls wanted to see us dance; the floor was cleared, and nothing would do, but we must dance. So we gave them a waltz, which elicited immense laughter. The Indians are a mirth loving race. About 2 o'clock the ball broke up.

South Shore Return to the Sault

Monday, July 20th.

We spent the forenoon in preparing to embark. We had a great deal to do, besides getting the boat and crew ready—there were many *leaves-taking* and *long adieus* to be attended to. At Dr. Borup's and Mr. Okes' we spent an hour or more; and the ladies at parting gave that squeeze of the hand which says, as plainly as a soft and yielding palm can speak it "would you could stay here forever." I spent a couple of hours among the Indian lodges trying to buy some stone pipes. They had no handsome ones; and parted with such as they had very reluctantly. An Indian will sell his wife with less compunction of conscience, than his red or black pipe. Two pretty girls entreated us to take them with us to Ste. Mary's. One of them is the prettiest Indian girl I ever saw. Her features were all animation and beauty. She speaks only in Chippewa, but her voice is music's self. I could have listened to her an hour with great delight. Her figure was much superior to that of ordinary European ladies. A little below the ordinary height, with full round limbs and well turned neck and shoulder, she was trim, light of feet and easy and graceful in every motion. I told her we had not room in the boat for them. She said we might leave her sister, and she would go alone. I could not say her *nay;* but told her to be at the boat an hour before noon. With a sparkling eye, she bounded away like a deer, to prepare for her voyage. I returned to the boat, and found it already much to my surprise after 11 o'clock. The boat was ready and a majority opposed to waiting for the poor Indian girl; and I was obliged to embark without her. I fancy I can see her as she starts on her way to the appointed place, her heart beating high with joy and gladness; and then I can see her turn from the deserted spot and drop a tear of silent grief and bitter disappointment, and hear her mutter a deep curse on the faithlessness of the Muck-wa. It was cruel. But there was no intention of disappointing her. Had she appeared in time we would have taken her on board with pleasure. We took a man who works his passage. With a crew of five men the old boat moves glibly. We reached the mouth of the Montreal and encamped before sunset. —Distance, 21 miles.

Tuesday, July 21st.

Left our encampment this morning at ½ past 2 o'clock, and ran to Black River (20 miles) before breakfast. We had a fair wind till 9 o'clock when it died away, and the heat was very oppressive until after sunset. The evening has been the warmest we have had this summer. We encamped early at the mouth of Iron River. Mr. Bell and his men were all absent. We found his wife and her mother sole inhabitants of the place. We have made a fine march to-day—one of the best since we entered the lake, and mostly by rowing. —Distance, 60 miles.

Wednesday, July 22nd.

This has been quite a stormy day, but without much rain. We embarked with a light wind from the S. S. W. which soon increased to such a rate that we considered it rather hazardous sailing. We went with it, however, at top speed until after 9 o'clock when we ran under the lee of a friendly point and remained between three and four hours. Thinking it a pity to lose the benefit of a westerly wind we took advantage of a pause in the storm and once more put to sea. But the wind soon raised and in a few minutes blew quite a gale. We were now unable to make shore. The breakers, for miles ahead were dashing their white crests against a rocky shore and covering the surface of the water with a sheet of foam. We continued on in this way about an hour, during which we must have run twelve miles, then turning a short rock point we ran into Graverod's River through a passage eight feet wide. We had scarcely landed when the fog became so dense that we could scarcely see a rod. If it had settled down upon us 20 minutes sooner, the Lord only knows where we should have found ourselves before night. Our running time to-day has been five hours. —Distance, 38 miles.

Thursday, July 23rd.

It was late this morning when we embarked. There was a thick curtain of fog hanging over the lake, whose bosom was still heaving with the deep emotions that so agitated her yesterday. But about 7 o'clock, when not a breath of air was stirring, the thick volumes of vapor began to roll up into the heavens, and in less than an hour we were broiling under an unclouded sun. We breakfasted at the [Keweenaw] Portage, and, while it was preparing, hunted on the beach for some of those beautiful carnelions which Schoolcraft in his Journal says are so abundant. Unfortunately we found none. From the Portage we continued our course along a sandy & gravelly beach about 15 miles, when a delightfully cool breeze came to our relief, and we glided along smoothly and comfortably until we reached our place of encampment. This is on the largest of five or six beautiful little islands which lie at the mouth of *Double,* or Pe-chau-grein Bay. This group lies off the west cape of the bay and, taken in connection with the peculiar shape of the bay itself presents a very fanciful appearance. —Distance to-day, 45 miles.

Friday, July 24th.

The entire forenoon was spent in gathering agates, and with such good success that we have concluded to give this bay the name of Agate Harbor. And an excellent harbor it is too—accessible at any time, and affording shelter from almost any wind. The rock which contains the agate is called amygdaloid and extends about a mile along the west side of the harbor. We worked a number of very good agates out of the solid rock; but, for want of a sledge or crowbar, were unable to break the rock sufficiently to get the large ones out whole. After working near an hour at a very fine one, I was obliged to leave it. I got one out weighing five or six pounds, but it was rather coarse. Some of the finest I obtained were picked up among the pebbs on the beach. At 1 o'clock we embarked; but, owing to a fresh eastern breeze, our progress was very slow. We stopped at

Copper Harbor to get five casks of minerals and leave two of provisions for the Doctor. This done we proceeded on to the Marais,[43] which I shall call Rock Harbor, & encamped. We have advanced to-day but 12 miles.

Saturday, July 25th.

On the extreme point of Keweenaw, seven or eight miles from our last place of encampment, we found a portion of the same rock which appears at Agate Harbor and picked up some very pretty specimens of agate; but they are by no means as plentiful here as at that place. We also found beautiful specimens of calcareous spar, crystalized quartz, radiated zeolite and chalcedony. In passing round the point we encountered a heavy dead swell that almost stopped our progress. Six or eight miles this side of the point we put nine casks of minerals into the company's storehouse, and found their room vastly more agreeable than their company. The sea, continuing quite high, we ran into the mouth of Tobacco River and encamped. I regret that I have not been able to witness the least examination of the copper veins this side the point. They are the same veins that were examined by Dr. Houghton eight years ago. We found the mark of a blast which he put in at that time, when we went up; and he has promised to give me a particular description when he returns. —Distance traveled to-day, 30 miles.

Sunday, July 26th.

From Tobacco River we followed down the coast six miles to a point opposite a small island called Traverse Island. From this point batteaux and canoes usually make a traverse to Point Abbaye. It is about 18 miles. The wind was from the east— the worst direction—and the fog so dense as to render the shore invisible at the distance of ¼ of a mile. Our men shook their heads and declared that the traverse had never been made in such weather. The Captain said he would not undertake to keep the course and quit the helm. We appointed Douglass Captain Pro. Tem. and told the men to ply their oars. We reached the [Traverse] island in safety a little over an hour and a half—having been out of sight of land most of the time.

---

[43]See note 36, page 45.

This is one-third of the way across. We took breakfast on the island and waited two hours for the fog to rise. But it continued thick as ever and we started on the remainder of the traverse —being 12 miles. This we accomplished in three hours. Another traverse of six miles brought us over the mouth of Huron Bay, three miles east of which we entered Huron River & encamped. It was perilous to attempt the traverse in such weather and the men, sensible of the danger almost rowed themselves to death. —Distance, 33 miles.

Monday, July 27th.

There has nothing occurred to-day to break the dull monotony of our voyage. A dead swell and light head wind met us at every point—nothing but row—row—row. We have passed successively Pine, Salmon Trout and St. John's Rivers, and are encamped at Granite Point on the bank of Garlic River. We spent a Sabbath at this place on our way up. The Point is a little remarkable as showing the junction of red sandstone, granite and trap. We estimate our day's work to be 35 miles.

Tuesday, July 28th.

This morning the atmosphere was perfectly clear. The air delightfully cool and fresh and the lake perfectly calm. We embarked a little after five o'clock, and had proceeded but a few miles when we were favored with a gentle sailing breeze that left us nothing more to wish for. The coast before us made a broad sweep inland, forming a bay [Presque Isle and Marquette Harbors] about 10 miles in depth and 25 in width. The elements all gave promise of so fair a day, that we were induced to make this large traverse, and steered direct for the farthest point. When about one-third of the way over the wind began to increase and continued to blow stronger and stronger, until we found ourselves flying along at steamboat speed and dancing over waves that looked, to our eyes, like little mountains. Fortunately the wind was dead astern, and with a reefed sail we were able to scud before it. It was impossible to land at any place on the beach, but we knew there was a good point ahead and laid our course for Grand Island. We reached the harbor a little before 2 P. M. having run *50 miles before breakfast.* Here we found Ankvim, Holmes and Chamberlin and their vessel,[44] men, women and children. The boat arrived here three days ago, and brought up a family of settlers by the name of Williams.[45] He is the first *actual settler* above the Sault Ste. Marie. There is not a better natural harbor in the world than Grand Island. The water is very deep in every part of the bay, there is a perfectly safe channel leading in both from the east and west, and it is so completely land-locked that a vessel scarcely needs her anchor. The shores are high and handsome, and have been cultivated by the Indians. The American Fur Company once had a post here.[46] H. A. Levake [Le Veque][47] spent several winters here. —Distance to-day 50 miles.

Wednesday, July 29th.

We have passed to-day two of the greatest natural curiosities of the lake; to wit; the Pictured Rocks and Grand Sables. The heavy swells from the lake breaking against the rocks formed a grand scene, but the back seas prevented our near approach to them. The motion of the boat also rendered it very difficult to make a good sketch. There are many places along there that would make a fine picture. The sketch, however,

---

[44]Their vessel was the schooner *Mary Elizabeth*. The three men could not be identified.

[45]Abraham Warren Williams (1792-1873) was born in Vermont and first came to the Lake Superior country about 1818, where he fished for a short time at Whitefish Point. He settled in Illinois and, in 1840, he sold his farm there and returned to Lake Superior intending to settle at Sault Ste. Marie. He found the frontier town ". . . too rough a place to bring up a family of children." (He eventually was the father of 12.) While at the Sault, he met O-mo-no-mo-nee, chief of the Grand Island Indians, who invited him to live with them on the island. Williams accepted, and his settlement on Grand Island became one of the most prominent on the south shore of Lake Superior.

[46]There are indications that a trading post was in operation on Grand Island in the late 1700's, and others intermittantly operated in succeeding years. The American Fur Co. built a post there at a time when it established six others on Lake Superior, according to the Act of Congress of May 26, 1824. The post apparently fell into disuse in the late 1830's; Abraham Williams utilized some of its abandoned buildings when he moved there in 1840.

[47]H. A. LeVeque may have been a clerk for the North West Co. Col. Thomas McKenney, a U. S. Indian agent who made a trip along the south shore of Lake Superior in 1826, noted that "The North West Trading Co. once had an establishment here [Grand Island]. Their clerk was a Frenchman. The Indians beset his establishment and resolved to take away his goods. He, beng unwilling to survive the odium of being vanquished, or the suspicion of having been accessory to the plunder, drew his pistol and shot himself." See McKenney's *Sketches of a Tour of the Lakes* (Baltimore: Fielding Lucas, Jr), 1827.

should be made with colored pencils in order to show something of the manner in which the rocks are painted. A little west of Miner's River there is a rock 175 feet high which stands out boldly into the lake. There are six or eight large caves in its base which communicate with each other so that the rock appears to be supported on pillars. The top is crowned by two towers. For want of a better, we gave it the name of Gothic Rock. Each of the party made a sketch. Half a mile east of the river the rock attains its greatest height. It was our intention to make an accurate measurement but the waves prevented a landing. This point of the rock is beautifully painted and shaped like the broadside of a large ship of war. Our estimates of its height varied from 250 to 350 feet. We affected a landing with much difficulty at La Chapelle, having passed and made a sketch of La Portaille.[48] This appears to me to be the grandest portion of the rocks. But for a mile or two east of La Chapelle, the scene is scarcely inferior to it. The painting of the rocks seems to have changed considerably since we went up. Their colours generally appeared less brilliant; and I have no doubt they are much brighter immediately after the spring rains than in the latter part of summer when the earth and rocks become hot and dry.

We reached the west end of the Sables, and, sending on the boat, ascended the steepest and highest portion of them. The west end is full 100 feet higher than the east. It is all of 350 feet. We walked the entire length and came to the conclusion that they extended six miles. At first view we were unwilling to call it three miles from one extreme to the other. Their greatest height makes the distance appear much less than it really is. This is peculiarly the case with the Pictured Rocks. Our boat seemed scarcely to move while passing them. Encamped at Grand Marais. —Distance to-day, 45 miles.

Thursday, July 30th.

We left Grand Marais this morning before 3 o'clock and arrived at White Fish Point an hour before sunset. The whole distance was performed without raising sail. One broad gravel beach, with sand near the water's edge, extends from the Marais

---

[48]The (Grand) Portal, or Doric Arch, collapsed in 1906.

to the Point. On the Point we found Capt. Keith and Capt. Roby of the Maumee Co.,[49] each with a party of fishermen and in good spirits. Roby has been there nearly a month and built quite a comfortable log house. Keith has also put up a temporary loggery; in truth the city has grown one-half since we were here before. As yet they have had ill success in fishing; but they are still strong in the faith, and expect to make fortunes in the fall. Capt. Roby has put about 50 barrels. A short time since he took 15 barrels in one day. Keith has been fishing but a day or two. He put up two barrels yesterday. It has been a very bad season for fishing so far, in all parts of the lake. The American Fur Company have not caught half as many as they did last summer by this time. I think every company here is in a fair way to lose money. 45 miles to-day.

Friday, July 31st.

Farewell, Lake Superior! We have shaken hands and parted in peace. We took a direct course from White Fish Point to Parisian Island 12 miles, thence to Gros Cap 18 miles and thence to Sault Ste. Marie 15 miles. A few miles this side of Gros Cap we met Maj. D. F. Hill, Dr. Clark and Mr. Chadfield,[50] all from Illinois, on their way to the head of the lake in a bark canoe, bound for the Mississippi. Maj. Hill had a letter to me; but the wind was drifting them back so fast that we could remain together but a short time. Their preparations for the voyage were made with great secrecy, and they intend to explore the copper region thoroughly. About five miles above the Sault we passed Point o'Pah—a delightful spot on the Canada side. It is the favorite place of resort of all the fashionable people who wish to escape the heat and dust and bustle of the city of

---

[49]These men and Maumee Co. could not be identified. Whitefish Point had been the scene of extensive commercial fishing over the years, and the Maumee Co. was obviously engaged in that business. It is believed to have been financed by an Ohio group, and, like many of the Whitefish Bay fishing operations, it was probably a short-lived, seasonal enterprise.

[50]Maj. D. F. Hill was a surveyor and landlooker from Illinois. In a letter in the archives of the Chicago Historical Society, written to Elias Kangham, dated January 9, 1835, James W. Stephenson of Galena, Illinois, noted that "Mr. D. F. Hill . . . is known to me to be a highly deserving young gentleman, and also to be a well qualified practical surveyor." The others mentioned by Penny could not be identified.

Sault Ste. Marie. We came down over the rapids in fine style, and landed amid the hearty cheers of our friends. Our encampment is on the green between the fort and town, and we may consider our Lake Superior voyage at a close. Distance, 45 miles.

* * *

TABLE OF DISTANCES

From	Detroit to Mackinaw	320
"	Mackinaw to Detour	45
"	Detour to Sault Ste. Marie	45
"	Ste. Marie to Gros Cap	15
"	Gros Cap to Point Iroquois	6
"	Point Iroquois to Tequimiminen River	25
"	Tequimiminen to White Fish Point	20
"	White Fish Point to Twin River	24
"	Twin River to Grand Marais	21
"	Grand Marais to LaChapelle	24
"	La Chapelle to Miner's River	8
"	Miner's River to Grand Island	7
"	Grand Island to Au Train River	8
"	Au Train River to Chocolate River	30
"	Chocolate River to River Des Morts	9
"	River Des Morts to Granite Point	5
"	Granite Point to Pine River	20
"	Pine River to Huron River	8
"	Huron River to Point Abbaye	6
"	Point Abbaye to L'Anse	24
"	L'Anse to Portage River	15
"	Portage River to Tobacco River	23

298   410

From	Tobacco River to Bay Du Gres	7
"	Bay Du Gres to Cascade River	7
"	Cascade River to Rock Harbor	12
"	Rock Harbor to Copper Harbor	4
"	Copper Harbor to Agate Harbor	8
"	Agate Harbor to the Portage	32

"   Portage to Misery River   22
"   Misery River to Ontonagon River   .   .   .   30
"   Ontonagon River to Iron River   .   .   .   15
"   Iron River to Presque Isle River   .   .   .   25
"   Presque Isle River to Carp River .   .   .   6
"   Carp River to Black River   5
"   Black River to Montreal River   .   .   .   22
"   Montreal River to La Point   21   514

Detroit to La Point   924

METEOROLOGICAL TABLE

1840		Mean Temperature	
June	Morning	48°	
	Noon	66°	Fahrenheit
	Sunset	54°	
July	Sunrise	60°	
	Noon	75°	
	Sunset	66°	

Extreme Variation

June	5th	38°
	23rd	85°
	30th	38°
July	1st	45°
	21st	85°
June	17 days	Fair
	3 "	Cloudy
	7 "	Rainy
	3 "	Showery
July	25 days	Fair
	2 "	Foggy
	3 "	Rainy
	1 day	Showery

APPENDIXES

Letter of Charles W. Penny to Mr. and Mrs. Archibald Penny

Mr. Archibald Penny
Elm Post Office
Putnam Co. N. Y.

Detroit, Monday, Oct. 29th, 1832

Dear Parents.

You will see by the date of this that I am once more in Michigan, and it becomes me with gratitude to acknowledge that I arrived here in safety and good health, having performed a long and tedious journey without accident or injury. But as I have not been here long enough to gather news of more importance, I will give you a brief history of my travels. After I left you, with apparent cheerfulness, our first stopping place was Poughkeepsie where we took dinner, and then ascended a hill south of the village to enjoy a prospect of the river. It was truly an interesting Scene. Twenty miles of the Hudson crowded with all kinds of vessels lay full in view. At length the Steam Boat *North America* made her appearance; we boarded her and soon lost sight of Poughkeepsie and everything in its vicinity. Our passage up the river was pleasant 'till we came to the over-slaugh where we were hindered some hours. It was near 8 o'clock in the evening when we landed at Albany, and, after some looking around as to what house we should spend the night in, we finally concluded to take lodgings on board a canal boat which was then just starting for Buffalo. We were all night and all the next day in going to Schenectady; but the numerous curiosities both natural and artificial to be seen on the route amply compensated us for the loss of time. We had a fine view of the C [illegible] falls, and you will recollect that the canal is carried over the Mohawk, twice on extensive arches which are curiosities that the hurried traveler never sees. From Schenectady our journey was slow yet uninterrupted. On Sunday the 21st we arrived at Lyons and left Edmund. We saw

Mr. Ruben Foster and family who were well. On Monday we stopped at Rochester and spent half the day in visiting the falls, mills and manufactories. The next day we left Mr. Bradley at Albion. But as our time seemed to pass unusually swift we thought it not advisable to stop with him and visit our acquaintance in the town of Barra. My friend Crosby and myself now proceeded alone. We arrived at Buffalo Wednesday morning, having traveled every inch of the canal, and took the Steam Boat *Enterprise* bound for Detroit. The weather was pleasant, but owing to a stiff breeze *dead-a-head,* our progress was so slow that it was 9 o'clock Thursday night before we reached Grand River. Here I left my last traveling companion, and here my troubles commenced. We left Grand River at midnight and before morning we came in contact with a Schooner. The shock was so sudden and violent that some of the passengers were thrown from their births to the cabin floor. The Schooner ran her bow into us just forward of the wheel house, which it nearly destroyed, broke in our poop deck and injured the wheel. But in return we carried away her bowsprit, bows, and all; then took her in tow and made the best of our way to Cleveland. There we stayed 24 hours to make temporary repairs. At 1 o'clock Saturday morning we again put to sea, and stood for Detroit. A head wind still made our progress slow, and finding our stock of wood too much reduced to carry us into Detroit, we ran into Put-in-Bay—the place where Perry took his fleet after his memorable engagement with the British.* It is the loveliest bay I ever saw, and if I had been a painter it would have been my delight to picture the scene. A company of us, 12 in number, took the small boat, went ashore on Put-in-Bay Island and visit a *cave,* the greatest curiosity I ever saw. The passage that led to it was very narrow between a ledge of rocks, but the cave itself was spacious, covering two acres of ground. We left the bay Saturday night and arrived here yesterday about noon. The boat is now ready to start and I must

---

*Penny is referring to the famous Battle of Lake Erie, September 10, 1813, during the War of 1812. Admiral Oliver H. Perry, in command of the flagship *Lawrence,* defeated the British fleet; his success marked the beginning of American superiority on Lake Erie and the battle was a major turning point of the war.

leave this hasty scratch by assuring you that I am well and in-
dulging the most ardent wishes that this may find you all in
good health.

I am with respect your
affectionate Son
Chas. W. Penny

APPENDIX B

Letter of Charles W. Penny to James K. Penny.

Mr. James K. Penny
Towner's Post Office
Putnam Co. N. Y.

Detroit, March 24, 1839

My Dear Brother,

I was truly gratified with your letter. You must accept my
best thanks, and try to deserve them by writing again. I suppose it is the first letter you ever wrote, and as such is very
creditable. Perhaps I am to blame for not writing to you before,
and thus give you an opportunity to derive the benefits of an
epistolary correspondence with one older and more experienced
than yourself. But you must remember that when I left home
you were but a child, and those who are absent never make
allowance for the growth of children. I should be happy to
correspond with you every week; and you may feel assured that
if you write often and regularly it will soon be an easy and
delightful task. You should take every opportunity to write to
Elijah and all your absent friends and acquaintances. It will be
a source of high and lasting improvement.

As an example, which I would recommend you to follow,
I will tell you what I am doing this winter. Myself and five
others formed an association—called the "Athenian Club." We
meet every Monday evening, and *three* of the club each read an
original *essay* on some particular subject. The other three read
criticisms both pleasant and profitable. I was writing an essay
for the next meeting when I received your letter, but I have laid
it aside for the greater pleasure of writing to you. Now, don't
be discouraged, or feel bad, or find fault with me, if I give you

a few gentle hints about writing. Your letter is all very good except the spelling. That part beats Jack Downing's best efforts all to nothing. On the first half of the first page I count *thirteen* words wrongly spelled. This is almost unpardonable in a young gentleman like yourself. You should have a dictionary by you when you write, and refer to it whenever you are at a loss how to spell a word. Your penmanship may be ever so beautiful and your sentences constructed according to the best rules of modern rhetoric, but if words of common use are misspelled it will spoil the whole of it. Nothing will teach you to spell correctly so quickly as writing, if you bestow due attention. I suppose the storm to which you allude was the same which passed over New York & Philadelphia with such disastrous fury. About the same time something of a hurricane visited this city, blowing down signs and old barns, but doing very little damage.

"The Maine War"* is our present great topic. People are much excited, and the arrival of every mail is an epoch in this goodly city. The British have a thousand redcoats nearly opposite, well supplied with the munitions of war, and in case of a declaration, could reduce Detroit to a heap of ashes in one night. You may well suppose we feel some anxiety to know whether we are to have war or not. If war comes there will be much hard fighting on this frontier. My own opinion is that Great Britain dare not fight the yankees now, and consequently that there will not be much trouble. Since the last of November, I have been in the U. S. service. So you see that according to Shakespeare, I have passed through the ages of infancy, childhood, &c., and am now the *"Soldier,* full of strange oaths, and bearded like a pard, seeking the bubble reputation even in the cannon's mouth." The Company to which I belong is large (80 in number) and well equipped. It would raise your little war spirit just to see us parade through the streets in our gay uniforms. If we have a war, and I should be shot—it will probably be announced in the *Detroit Daily Advertiser* thus—"The Brady Guards led the charge and behaved with great gallantry; they

---

*In 1838, American and Canadian lumberjacks began moving into the Aroostook River region, which was in a long-disputed boundary area between Maine and New Brunswick. An ensuing brawl between the two groups, known as the Maine or Aroostook War, seriously strained U. S.-British relations.

77

broke through the enemy's line, and took two batteries by storm. Fifteen of their number were either killed or wounded. Among the former, we regret to learn, was Sergeant Penny, who fell while bravely fighting for his own and country's liberty."

My health is very good this Spring; and I think, after my business is closed up, I shall take some comfort in traveling. I intend to visit Patterson, but cannot say how soon, or how long I shall stay. I cannot afford to be idle a great while.

I should like to know what you have been doing this winter, whether you have been to school, feeding cattle & chopping wood or loitering away your time with the boys & girls of the neighborhood. Either is good business if well followed but you must "keep your eye skinned taut" when you begin to tamper with the girls, or they will play the duce with your upper works. Write immediately when you receive this. Give my warmest love to all our friends, and don't forget to ask them for a short letter.

Tell father I saw Uncle Hiram last week. He gave me a full statement of his affairs. He has been unfortunate, but I think will be able in a few years to meet all his engagements. I rather think he will marry this summer. He has got his eye on a fine young widow whose amiable temper and kindness of heart are her chief recommendations.

Your affectionate friend & Brother
Chas. W. Penny

APPENDIX C

Letter of Charles W. Penny to the Editor of the
JACKSON (MICH.) DAILY CITIZEN

LETTER FROM MARQUETTE

A Trip on Lake Superior — The Southern Shore 26 years ago — The Copper Mines — Hancock — Marquette — Holyoke Silver Lead Mines — Visitors — Bishop McCrosky.

Marquette, July 28, 1866

Mr. Editor:

"An oft told tale," if a good one, is very agreeable to the writer. A trip on Lake Superior has been so often the theme of letter writers that writing about it has become a habit. And were it possible to convey to your readers the refreshing coolness of the breezes, the sense of exquisite enjoyment, or the appetite for food which one experiences in these regions, they would be grateful to the writer for the feeblest attempt to describe them. I have little to say of the beautiful and varied scenery of the route hither, except that it compels the attention to such a degree that one lays aside the romance and poetry found in books, loses all taste for games and common-place conversation, and even robs himself of some hours of sleep to view the changing shores and ever interesting waters. When fairly embarked upon the voyage the first sensation is that of repose. Cares, toils, vexations, and disappointments have flown away. Corporeal evils are left on shore. Simply to be, to have existence, seems the realization of all the blessings of life. But the stomach, that faithful inward monitor, soon reminds him that he has wants; and by the third day he is aware that meals are distressingly far apart, and he begins to fear that white fish may not appear on table at the next sitting. "Good digestion waits on appetite" here without special invitation.

I coasted the southern shore of this lake 26 years ago. It was then an unbroken wilderness, save one solitary trading post, far from the borders of civilization; and little did I think I should live to see on it so many populous towns, with large, well-filled hotels, schoolhouses and churches, mining villages, stamp mills, smelting works, with steam ferries and steamboats plying between them. Immense sums of money have been expended; and one regrets to see in abandoned shafts and deserted warehouses evidence that much of it brought no return.

The most productive copper mines at present are those near Houghton and Hancock. These towns are on opposite sides of the western arm of Portage Lake, which there, and for several miles farther west, is about 60 rods wide. The shores rise abruptly to a height of a 1,000 feet, and the two villages, built on these steep declivities, seem very ambitious to overlook each other. Hancock, on the north side, is most aspiring, crowned with derricks and the smoke of engines, commanding one of the most picturesque and beautiful views, where all is beautiful.

Marquette, however, my old favorite, fully sustains its reputation as the best town on the lake. It has a substantial prosperity, and an air of permanence. Many improvements in its streets and public and private buildings have been made within a year. The Catholics and Baptists have each built fine churches, and the Episcopal church has been enlarged and adorned at a cost of over $7,000. It is now the handsomest church of its size I have ever seen.

Yesterday I went fifteen miles into the depth of "the forest primeval," to visit the "Holyoke"—the nearest of the Silver Lead Mines.* Mr. B. L. Livermore—nephew to Fidus Livermore, of our city—the Superintendent, received us with generous hospitality—first providing a sumptuous dinner, and then showing us through every part of the mine. It is situated on the northeast ¼ of Section 2, Township 48, North, Range 27 West. The vein averages seven feet in width, and crops out on the top of a steep bluff 150 feet high. A tunnel of 350 feet, now nearly completed, will strike the vein 150 feet below the surface. A shaft following the dip of the vein has been sunk about 40 feet, and about 100 tons of vein matter—quite rich in mineral—thrown out. It bids fair in a few years to make silver one of the articles of Michigan exports. But a large pile of greenbacks must be expended first.

Hotels and boarding houses here are all well filled with visitors. There are several families here from Tennessee, Kentucky and Chicago, spending the summer. Among them is Mr. Wilson, of the *Chicago Journal,* who has built a charming cottage on the bay, in a grove of pines, and laid out his grounds in a tasty manner, on which are a fish pond, fountain, bowling alley, &c. Marquette is already a fashionable watering place. Ladies are as much given to riding, dressing and dancing, as at Saratoga or Newport.

Bishop McCroskey arrived yesterday, and will preach tomorrow and administer the rite of confirmation in the evening.

Yours, &c.,

C. W. P.

---

*The Holyoke Silver Mine was located six miles directly north of the city of Ishpeming, on the north side of what is now the Dead River Storage Basin.

(NOTE: Charles W. Penny and Lewall L. Vaughn, also of Jackson, invested in real estate in Marquette in 1858, and in 1859, platted Penny & Vaughn's Addition to the City of Marquette.)

BIBLIOGRAPHY

Annual Report of the American Historical Association, 1944. Vols. II & III, *Calendar of the American Fur Company's Papers.* Washington, D. C.: United States Government Printing Office, 1945.

Bradish, Alvah. *Memoir of Douglass Houghton.* Detroit: Raynor & Taylor, Printers, 1889.

Carter, Clarence E. *The Territorial Papers of the United States.* Vols. XI & XII, *The Territory of Michigan.* Washington, D. C.: United States Government Printing Office, 1945.

Castle, Beatrice Hanscom. *The Story of Grand Island.* Munising, Mich.: 1906. Unpublished manuscript in the collection of the J. M. Longyear Research Library, Marquette, Mich.

Catlin, George B. *The Story of Detroit.* Detroit: The Detroit News, 1923.

Hubbard, Bela. *Memorials of a Half-Century.* New York: G. P. Putnam's Sons, 1887.

MacCabe, Julius P. Bolivar. *Directory of the City of Detroit, 1837.* Detroit: William Harsha, 1837. Facsimile reproduction by R. L. Polk & Co., Detroit, 1937.

Michigan Biographies. Vols. I & II. Lansing: Michigan Historical Commission, 1924.

Michigan Pioneer & Historical Collections. Lansing: Robert Smith Printing Co., 1904.

Moore, Charles. *History of Michigan.* Chicago: Lewis Publishing Co., 1915.

"Notes & Documents," *Michigan History Magazine,* XXXI (Sept., 1947), pp. 344-345.

Nute, Grace Lee. *Lake Superior.* New York: The Bobbs-Merrill Co., 1944.

Rintala, Edsel K. *Douglass Houghton.* Detroit: Wayne University Press, 1954.

Schoolcraft, Henry R. *Narrative Journal of Travels.* Albany, N. Y.: E. & E. Hosford, 1821.

Wood, Edwin O. *Historic Mackinac.* New York: The Macmillan Co., 1918.

INDEX

82